NEW DIRECTIONS IN THEATRE

General Editor JULIAN HILTON

NEW DIRECTIONS IN THEATRE

Published titles

FEMINISM AND THEATRE
Sue-Ellen Case

IMPROVISATION IN DRAMA
Anthony Frost and Ralph Yarrow

PERFORMANCE
Julian Hilton

NEW DIRECTIONS IN THEATRE
Julian Hilton (*editor*)

TRANSPOSING DRAMA
Egil Törnqvist

Forthcoming titles

GENDER AND THEATRE
Susan Bassnett

POSTMODERNISM AND PERFORMANCE
Nick Kaye

THEATRE AS ACTION
Lars Kleberg

REPRESENTATION AND THE ACTOR
Gerry McCarthy

SEMIOTICS OF THE DRAMATIC TEXT
Susan Melrose

New Directions in Theatre

Edited by

JULIAN HILTON

150th YEAR

MACMILLAN

First published in Great Britain 1993 by
THE MACMILLAN PRESS LTD
Houndmills, Basingstoke, Hampshire RG21 2XS
and London
Companies and representatives
throughout the world

A catalogue record for this book is available
from the British Library

ISBN 0-333-39291-4 hardcover
ISBN 0-333-39292-2 paperback

Printed in Hong Kong

Contents

General Editor's Preface

In the past ten years, Theatre Studies has experienced remarkable international growth, students seeing in its marriage of the practical and the intellectual a creative and rewarding discipline. Some countries are now opening school and degree programmes in Theatre Studies for the first time; others are having to accommodate to the fact that a popular subject attracting large numbers of highly motivated students has to be given greater attention than hitherto. The professional theatre itself is changing, as graduates of degree and diploma programmes make their way through the 'fringe' into established theatre companies, film and television.

Two changes in attitudes have occurred as a result: first, that the relationship between teachers and practitioners has significantly improved, not least because many more people now have experience of both; secondly, that the widespread academic suspicion about theatre as a subject for study has at least been squarely faced, if not fully discredited. Yet there is still much to be done to translate the practical and educational achievements of the past decade into coherent history, and this series is intended as a contribution to that task. Its contributors are chosen for their combination of professional and didactic skills, and are drawn from a wide range of countries, languages and styles in order to give some impression of the subject in its international perspective.

This series offers no single programme or ideology, yet all its authors have in common the sense of being in a period of transition and debate out of which the theory and practice of theatre cannot but emerge in a new form.

JULIAN HILTON

Bausch, Chereau and Mnouchkine are making their mark outside continental Europe, and the work of Peter Brook no longer seems as radically remote from the mainstream of English-language theatre as it once did.

Performance studies

All this however, does not explain the surge in popularity of theatre studies in schools and colleges, especially in the English-speaking world. Degree courses are vastly oversubscribed; the teaching of English more and more demands skills in practical theatre; drama is no longer the annual ritual of the school Shakespeare, Gilbert and Sullivan or, more recently, Lloyd-Webber. The simplest explanation of this popularity lies in the attention theatre studies pays to affective as well as cognitive learning. The whole body (brain and all) is included in the educational process, and there is simultaneous emphasis on process (rehearsal, practical skills) and product (performance, interpretation). This is no more than a reassertion of humanist values that emerged in parallel to the theatrical Renaissance, the values of integrated and integrative learning. Learning, as perceived through performance, is a communal, part-applied, part-pure, discipline. It depends on individual resources, but also on individual contributions to group efforts: what is learned is digested both by the head and by the heart.

One major factor in the rise of Renaissance theatre was the advance in educational standards in the sixteenth century, and the great majority of playwrights profited immeasurably from the new concern for education. It was understood that advances in culture required investment in education. At the same time, the great new intellectual vistas opened by figures such as Copernicus, Erasmus, Luther and Calvin delivered the playwrights intimations of new worlds which they in their plays could explore. Theatre had the function of a cultural and historical laboratory, evaluating the past in terms of the present in great cycles of plays, such as Shakespeare's histories. The past was reconstructed as present myth. Much of the vigour of the new plays came from the appropriation into metaphor of the new technologies and the new conceptual attitudes. Shakespeare constantly uses books, the expanding world and the new Copernican cosmology as a basis for metaphor. He even called his theatre the Globe.

New directions

A similar potential has been opened to theatre in our time, especially in the appropriation of theories such as that of relativity, with its radical explosion of fixed notions of space and time, to develop a metaphoric structure quite distinct from the necessary logic of the classical play as observed by Aristotle. The notions of plot as linear, logical, causally determined, or of character as moral, exemplary, didactic, or even of message (or recoverable meaning) as immanent truth, are all cast in doubt. Adjusting to such rich potential will not be swift or easy. Voltaire distinguishes between acts of discovery of new terrain and acts of surveying that terrain; the one is at the frontiers of the known, the other at the frontiers of the understood. At this stage we are still slowly discovering the new shape of the world.

Hence the title: *New Directions*. In a way, the map of the world has to be redrawn, and with it a whole set of new bearings plotted. The chapters of this book are designed to help theatre practitioners and theatre-goers, if not yet started, to begin the process of reorientation, or to experiment with our investigative and practical models as enrichments or alternatives to their own. The book offers no consensus as to what are the principal concerns for the future, or about how best to deal with them. The common thread is the conviction that performance is a central concern in all contemporary cultural experience and speculation, whether at the personal level (how we 'perform' ourselves – that is, consciously make the most of our own abilities and opportunities) – or at the level of social interaction (understanding social processes in which we are engaged as akin to performance acts).

Part of our strategy is to make theoretical advances made in parallel disciplines available to the theatre. The field of textual hermeneutics may be opened up, as Elinor Shaffer argues (Ch. 6), to theatre practice, and such figures as Stanislavski may be located within an essentially hermeneutic tradition of interpretation. Patrice Pavis (Ch. 3), one of the leading exponents of semiotic theory, examines ways of combining the study of theatre as sign system with the reception processes implicit in the *mise-en-scène*. Denis Calandra (Ch. 2) takes more of an outsider's view of reception theory and locates it within the study of acts of performance, translation and adaptation in theatre as analogous modes of interpretation.

The role of Shakespeare as resource and model has a central part in Calandra's (as in Elinor Shaffer's) argument, in this instance in relation to a detailed analysis of a classic modern work, Heiner Müller's *Hamlet Machine*, whose very title challenges the integration of Shakespearian and post-Shakespearian, pre- and post-industrial theatrical attitudes. Heinz Fischer (Ch. 4) examines anthropological evidence in explaining the function of performance for an audience and seeks connections between the thesis of Frazer's *Golden Bough* and the neuro-physiological investigations of the Munich theatre-research team led by Heribert Schälzsky. Can audience behaviour best be explained by reference to mythic structures or by measurable physical needs? Anthony Gash (Ch. 5) takes a different view of the audience–performer relationship through a study of carnivalesque texts and modes of performing. Theatre is central to a process of social and societal release, through reversals of the norm and challenges, of a licensed kind, to existing hierarchies. This enables him to argue a continuity of performed experience from the pre-historical to the present.

Part of our strategy is to open up issues altogether new to theatre studies, such as the relationship between theatre and knowledge. This is discussed in Chapter 7 ('The Concept of Dialogue'), where connections are sought between theatrical dialogue and dialogue as a means of advancing understanding as a whole. Finally, in Chapter 8 the relationship between theatre and artificial intelligence (AI), is discussed.

The enlightened performer

When I referred to the increasing influence of the continental European on the English-language theatre, I mentioned the names of some of its most successful directors. This may seem obvious enough, yet the very mention of directors highlights a conservative element in the new theatre. Part of the point of trying to make available the possibilities opened by advances in critical theory is to liberate the performer from the tyranny of the director. To use a familiar phrase from the Enlightenment, it is now up to the performer to have once more the courage of his or her own intelligence, neither needing nor having to rely on a director to be told what a text means. This is asking for a realisation in performance practice of the principle of parallelism, a recognition that it is many voices, not just one, that now carry meaning, and meaning itself is dynamic, shifting. But it is, equally, time for a return to the spirit of medieval and Renaissance theatre, in

which the performer and what was performed were the end and the
beginning of performance.

The performance text?

Paradoxically, this latter, apparently conservative demand is the precondition for structural innovation in performance of the most challenging kind, the emancipation from any necessary relationship with
a 'text', the pursuit of improvisation. Aware of a gap between the
printed and the performed work, and increasingly concerned by the
extent of the divergence between print and performance, some critics
have tried to describe the performed work as the performance 'text'.
But, if performance is not to be described as a text, what then?

We may consider performance diagrammatically as the product of
a triangular set of forces – the performer, the space, and the time:

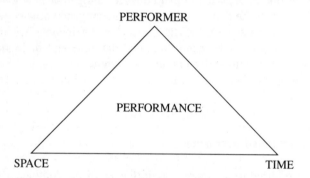

This model deliberately omits both any mention of a 'text', for two
principal reasons. First, there are key performance modes, such as
mime, which have no text at all – mime is iconic, text symbolic.
Secondly, even where a source text exists, in performance it is sub-
sumed into the whole. Likewise there is no formal mention of an
audience, for the reason that performers can perform without an
audience being present, however absurd regular performance of this
kind would be.

In *The Poetics* Aristotle establishes a hierarchy of factors in tragedy, as follows: plot, character, message/thought, diction, melody,
spectacle.[1] This effectively enables him to argue that what happens in
tragedy exists independent of the performed event and hence to make
spectacle an optional element in tragedy. In my companion volume in

this series, *Performance*, I criticise this position in detail, so I shall not rehearse all the arguments here. What matters is the central contention that in the theatre any plot or action exists only in the moment of performance and has no stable meaning or identity outside of the performance process. This in turn means that there is no single or necessary definition of what plot or action is, even in the case of a play with an authoritative source 'text', for every performance redefines, however marginally, the nature of the performed. The purpose of performing thus becomes one of generating an intensified experience for all who participate in it rather than the representation of some pre-existing action or state of feeling according to some immanent ideal located in its poetic, textual source.

Making the play

This permits us to come back, from a different perspective, to the omission of the audience from the diagram, for, seen in the terms I have just stated, the audience are as much 'performers' as the on-stage actors; indeed, what distinguishes theatrical performance from video or film, the main audio-visual alternatives, is its liveness, its openness to participation. In a quite literal sense, the audience co-operate in the performance: they do not merely collude in a willing suspension of disbelief. In fact, disbelief need not be suspended at all. The audience make the performance with the performers. Their presence acts as an intensificatory force, concentrating and legitimating the real activities and experiences of the performers. Which takes us to the next point.

Much is made of theatre as a representational art, as a sort of fiction, as licensed cultural hypocrisy. But this is to confuse effect and cause. The performance process may seem to be based on the willing assumption of false identities and false enthusiasm by the performers and collusion in the falsity by the audience. For this very reason Plato advocated banishment of dramatic poets from the ideal republic.[2] But the seeming hypocrisy is merely a precondition for performance and as such has in fact no, or what anthropologists call 'zero', value. Without an assumption of seemingly alien identity the 'performance' cannot begin; but, once assumed, that identity actually reveals itself as part of real, not a fictional, process. This is so because of the overall context of relativity in which space, time and identity itself are dynamic, not static, in nature; thus an actor cannot be feigning or lying when taking on the role of another, for that other role is no more nor less than another potential or actual part of his dynamic self. Not that this perception is new: Shakespeare's analysis of the world as a stage encompassed quite effortlessly the dynamic notion of the self, one man in his time playing many parts.

This raises in turn the question of play, and the relationship between 'play' and 'a play', or, more broadly, the relationship between cultural and personal behaviour and theatre. Aristotle rightly pointed out that there is a connection between the cultural urge to perform and learning through playing and imitating.[3] We learn by playing the roles and emotions of others, which in the very process become our own. In our own century child psychologists such as Jean Piaget[4] have shown that play is actually part of a sophisticated process of acquiring models of social behaviour, which we in part assimilate, in part adapt to suit our own needs. We may go one step further and point out that rehearsal for 'a play' is a particular version of the play process, where in a combination of assimilating a 'text' and adapting it to our own purposes in an act of interpretation we exactly repeat the child's process of action learning through playing – the one difference being that we are conscious of what we are doing. The emphatic play of a child becomes a more complex combination of empathy (getting into a part) and sympathy (representing it) in the adult. In this latter, adult model, action, or performance, is what emerges from the dialectic of empathy and sympathy, of being and representing, which may vary very widely from performance to performance.

The play of will

This variation points to another factor in the popularity of performance identified by thinkers from a wide variety of disciplines: for in performance is seen a model of choice patterns, or, put more traditionally, the exercise of the (free) will. In performance, the will is constantly capable of asserting itself, and, even when it does not, this is a chosen refusal, rather than a necessary one. Or that is the ideal. The performer who surrenders to directorial will surrenders with it his (or her) own intelligence and his own right of intervention in the individual performance. Naturally enough, even in modern democracies the habits of obedience are so schooled in us that the thought of disobedience in itself causes disquiet. No doubt because theatre has always been felt to be disobedient (i.e. in the exercise of its will to change the existing to something else), it has for centuries been at best tolerated and at worst cast out. But in the exercise of his own intelligence the performer is actually giving expression to his will, and thus, in what is a quite classical, Aristotelian manner, affirming the contribution of his performance to the politics of daily existence and the daily pursuit of meaning.

The relationship between performance and power as mediated through the performing will has been a subject of concern to thinkers since Plato. Plato's response to the problem was to banish the creators of drama. Aristotle's response was to invoke the power of the universal as the centre of all human activity, and in so doing he effectively set the terms of the debate about theatre in Western culture as it has been conducted ever since.[5] We know that, in practice, political leaders have always trained their appearances, and in the new audio-visual age performance skills turn out to be crucial to political success. When Brecht portrays Arturo Ui being trained to walk and talk like Julius Caesar, he is demonstrating how the political process as whole can be understood as a performance, a lesson not lost on contemporary politicians. In a quite straightforward way, performance is *Realpolitik*, the art of management of people and resources within time, to a given if unpredictable end.

Drama as genre?

The intervention of the performing will in the moment of performing has another profound effect on our understanding of 'drama'. It is traditional in studies of plays to classify them into genres, such as comedy, tragedy, history. In the overall study of literature, 'drama' is classified, with the novel and poetry, as one of the literary genres. But there are numerous difficulties in sustaining this view. Few plays fit neatly into any single category, and as a result curious critical bastards, such as 'comic relief', or 'problem plays', are fathered to sustain the generic case. The distinction between poetry and the novel, hard enough to sustain in any event, looks meaningless in 'drama', which can include both prose and poetry in the same work, and on occasion be wholly visual in character, a set of moving pictures, utterly non-literary. But, most significant, the factor which makes performance so distinctive, its continuous exercise of conscious choice, militates against the classification of any work as conforming to a particular genre, with predetermined rules of composition. If performance is to be accommodated within the concept of genre, it in the sense that each new performance carries within it the potential of a new genre, a claim that may of course equally well be advanced for any new work of art.

Legitimation

If it is not in its fidelity to or even deliberate breach of a generic norm that the value of performance may be measured, if there is this constant exercise of will, how then can we determine what effect a performance is having? The answer lies in what the German philosopher Habermas calls the process of *legitimation*,[6] which in turn is intrinsically bound up with the concept of *rehearsal*. What this means in essence is that the process whereby a given society makes decisions about itself, about its laws and politics, applies equally to performance. A decision is legitimated if under prevailing conditions it appears successfully to mediate between competing understandings of what the problem is and how to solve it. Rehearsal is nothing but this process of legitimation in miniature, in which decisions are taken on a provisional basis, tested and explored, then adopted more permanently or rejected.

What is so exhilarating is the speed of decision-making and the sense of emancipation from constraints which the ability rapidly to change a decision engenders; but in the past theatre has frequently denied itself this great liberty. In the effectively empty space of the Shakespearian Globe the performer was the most significant force, but in the Baroque theatre of elaborate sets and complex machines the sheer logistics of set-building and the pressures of soaring theatre costs progressively reduced the performer to the least significant force on stage. Performance became the business of accommodating the performers to the inflexible constraints of the performance environment, not of providing them with optimum performance conditions. Thus the whole concept of theatrical legitimacy became based on the extent to which rules of composition and performance (such as the unities) were mastered, if on occasion overcome. Legitimacy was subject to legislation, orthodoxy, autocracy: where the King sat was *de facto* the best view, and also the *right* view.

It was Richard Wagner's theatre in Bayreuth that perhaps more than any other began the long process of freeing performance from the autocratic constraints of the Baroque theatre building, though, perhaps inevitably, this act of liberation was matched by an emphasis on the single creative will (the start of director's theatre). Thus, at least in the short term, the losses balanced the gains. Brecht likewise developed a paradoxically emancipated and tyrannical theatre, in that his dramaturgy recognised the limitations of Wagner's *Gesamtkunstwerk*, with its purely aesthetic legitimation, but imposed in its place a form of politicised theatre that no more admitted the relativity of meaning than *The Ring*.

The new dramaturgy

This overall problem of legitimation led, eventually, to Peter Brook's call in *The Empty Space*[7] for a dramaturgy beyond Brecht and Beckett, beyond the legitimation of politics or of atomised poetry. This series of books is intended as a contribution to the development of that new dramaturgy, which must account for at least the five following principles of performance.

1   *Liveness*: theatre must grasp that its essential character is to be live, therefore to be exploratory, unmechanical.
2   *Participation*: however defined, the difference between sitting in front of a screen and facing a live actor consists in the opportunity for co-operation and collaboration with an audience.
3   *Improvisation*: following naturally from liveness and participation, which create different conditions for every performance. The true character of performance is improvisatory, even when based on an existing text. That is, the test of a performance is the extent to which it feels as though it could at any time take any direction, that in any given performance the outcome of *Macbeth*, for instance, could actually be different from the text's. When it is not, it is all the more shocking.
4   *Legitimation*: theatre is integral to social behaviour and simultaneously tests and is tested by the process of social legitimation. It offers a continuous critique of the real, and is in turn challenged by the real to go beyond the already legitimated, to envisage the innovatory. As such, it is a real not a fictional art, using certain formal procedures to traverse the threshold of legitimacy.
5   *Manifest will*: the innovative power of theatre rests on its ability

to manifest what in the wider reality is not possible or not yet imagined. It becomes therefore a place where the will can be manifest and thus a place of colossal potential energy, which may spill, kinetically, into wider political processes into possible worlds.

NOTES

1. Aristotle, *The Poetics*, trs. with critical notes and intro. by S. H. Butcher (London, 1936) p. 25.
2. Plato, *The Republic*, trs. with an intro. by H. D. P. Lee (Harmondsworth, Middx, 1955) pp. 383–6.
3. Aristotle, *The Poetics*, p. 15.
4. Jean Piaget, *The Moral Judgement of the Child*, trs. Marjorie Gabain (London, 1932) passim.
5. Aristotle, *The Poetics*, p. 89.
6. Jürgen Habermas, *Legitimation Crisis*, trs. Thomas McCarthy (London, 1976).
7. Peter Brook, *The Empty Space* (London, 1968) p. 63.

Chapter 2

The Aesthetics of Reception and Theatre

DENIS CALANDRA

Theatre, we all know, is a place where looking (and sometimes seeing) occurs. The Greek root of 'theatre' (from a verb meaning 'to see') tells us as much, and what Greek pictorial artists were inscribing in the fifth century BC, when they first began to value the spectator in their depictions of mythical and other events, has always been the embodied knowledge of anyone ever occupied with performance: a key structural feature of the art is the dynamic which obtains among participants in a 'theatre event', including those performing and otherwise making it happen, and those just 'out there' collectively and privately shaping it in their own fashion(s), as 'productive spectators'. What all 'reception commentators' have in common[1] – and this would include at one point or another a spectrum of theorists, ranging from semiotic gridmakers to deconstructers of all persuasions – is an inclination to account for the recipient's part in the complex web which constitutes art as a (more or less) 'communicative' sign.[2] At one extreme the recipient, the reader or, in our case, audience seems reduced to a kind of thinking flange; at the other, inflated to an undifferentiated mass of subjectivity.[3] Patrice Pavis, who knows a thing or two about theatre, sees the need in his semiological 'game of Chinese boxes' for reception theory: 'In fact, the performance text, the metatext of the *mise-en-scène* . . . can only be understood in the light of the different mechanisms (perceptual, emotive, textual and ideological) of reception.'[4] He does not go on to sketch the mechanisms in any detail, and it is symptomatic of the enormity of the problems encountered when one begins to ponder just exactly what 'reception' means that Pavis approaches a resignation before the effort. As for accounting historically for 'theatre events', he notes that 'reception of the performance becomes an act of which all critical trace is lost'.[5] References by Pavis and other theorists to the work of German scholar Hans Robert Jauss are significant in this context, specifically references to his concept of the 'horizon of expectations' as a factor in the reception of the literary object. The horizon idea, not original to Jauss, was formulated in a late-sixties attempt to reinvigorate literary history, and appears 'to refer to an intersubjective system or structure of expectations, a "system of references" or a mind-set that a hypothetical individual might bring to any text'.[6] Jauss was interested in tracing the mediation between the object's private inception and public reception. In the case of theatre's unwieldy polytextuality, the 'private inception' idea would have to be adapted to account for collective factors in creation and reception. There are horizons which belong to the text (at the unique moment of its creation, in its reception history) and horizons which belong to the readers, all modified by each other on a historical continuum. The question-and-answer of past and present preoccupies Jauss at this early stage, indicating his hermeneutical foundations. Jauss considered the manner of fusion of these horizons (formed of norms, knowledge of life, of art, and so on) significant, with value attached to work which effects some change or adjustment of norms, social or aesthetic, in readers. A critical problem with theatre, of course, is the disappearance of all but the mechanically reproduced traces (though these should not be ignored) of the 'performance text'. Historically, the only exceptions would be those non-Western traditions in which aspects of performance are consciously preserved – but here Jauss's parameter of norm-change would not apply. In our experience, just think of *one* actor co-creating *one* role, and the problems encountered. We might say that flashes of all the Shakespeare roles Gielgud ever played went into the conception of Edward Bond's Shakespeare persona in his play *Bingo*, which then left their indelible mark on Gielgud's (resistant, as I saw it) playing of the role written for him – a dubious bard. But how can this be recorded, much less achieve validity beyond assertion in mapping performance text history? Paul de Man describes Jauss's programme for literary history in technical terms as 'syntagmatic displacement within a synchronic structure becom[ing], in its reception, a paradigmatic condensation within a diachrony.'[7] The performance, seen first against its vast performance field (including behavioural, social 'performance' modes), is then perceived in significant series: with *so* many variables and nothing even as concrete as a literary artefact to hold on to, it all seems too impossibly neat for whirligig theatre, where everything, including the spectator, is in motion all the time. In the end, even Jauss turned his attention to the history of aesthetic experience, and a revaluing of aesthetic pleasure, which included reception as only one of its three modes.

With the polytextual 'theatre event' we are dealing with more than just a string of synchronies such as the course of the season, the 'run' (up to a point), the current media field, the cultural–social setting, the rehearsal activity, and so on. These interrelate (where there are playscripts) with the history of the script (its status as a 'classic'), the history of the roles/performers/*mises-en-scène* (readings with or against the grain), the history of the stage institution, the norms and conventions of performers as they coincide and/or conflict with behavioral norms of society – and so the list could go on, it seems, for ever. At the end of his book *Languages of the Stage* Pavis constructed 'An Exercise in Self-Exorcism' and asked himself revealing questions about reception and the 'discovery' of the creativity of the spectator and the transfer to the receptor of the belief in unlimited creativity, subjectivity and relativism. The plurality of readings and the dynamic and provisional situation of the field of study appeals to Pavis, who whimsically refers to Barthes's notion of the semiologist as an 'artist in disguise'.[8] The pleasure of creation, so he hints, supersedes the compulsion for semiological analysis. If one considers rehearsal procedures, which do sustain themselves as extensive periods of productive/creative watching by a specialized primary audience, what Pavis is getting at seems a natural enough development.

Way back in 1964 in *Elements of Semiology*, Barthes mused on the possibility of rediscovering a non-signifying object, imagining a utensil 'absolutely improvised' and with no similarity to an existing model. He pointed to Lévi-Strauss and the idea that tinkering was itself a search for meaning. 'Improvised' is the key word here, 'absolute improvisation', which of course, does not exist but which has not stopped people chasing it in theatre for centuries: maybe the experience of the chasing *is* the work of art in the long run. Barthes's search for the structures of meaning took him on a journey through semiology and beyond, where he 'textualised' the very reader the German reception analysts were trying to place in the topographies of culture, history, and the literary canon. Sontag points out that 'notions of theatre inform, directly or indirectly, all Barthes' work'.[9] Another informing notion, also of no little importance to Barthes's principal theatrical source, Brecht, was of course *pleasure*. *Spass, Genuss, plaisir, jouissance*: worlds of difference but a common denominator. Barthes fantasised about 'an aesthetic based entirely on the *pleasure of* the consumer, whoever he may be, to whatever class, whatever group he may belong, without respect to culture or language'.[10]

Jauss cites Freud, who shows the 'insight that in the psychic economy, purely aesthetic pleasure has a farther-reaching function which is that of "fore-pleasure" or an "incentive bonus"', disguised to 'make possible the release of still greater pleasure arising from deeper psychical sources'.[11] The inner distance (here the reference is also to Proust's remembrance) from a self that has become alien is abolished; self-enjoyment is connected to the enjoyment of what is other. The meanings which inhere in the German verb root for pleasure, *geniessen*, 'participation and appropriation', and the balance between disinterested contemplation and testing participation as a mode of experiencing oneself in a possible being-other, which Jauss sees opened up by the aesthetic attitude, has a relevance to theatre. It is always the presence of the others out there and, just maybe, *in* there that fascinates in theatre. That's why we show up – to be looked at or into, maybe seen through, or to do the looking and seeing ourselves.

In one of his comments on theatre history, Jauss uses religious plays of the Christian Middle Ages as an example of immediate aesthetic pleasure, claiming that even Augustine (inadvertently) confirms the power of aesthetic pleasure: 'More than a merely contemplative attitude of enjoyment is expected from the spectator of a religious play . . . he is no mere spectator who is separated from the scene by curtain and apron but someone who is drawn into an action. . . .'[12] This is considered a threshold in the history of aesthetic experience. To the medieval Christian, it would seem, the 'Thou of his God' out there is appropriated through the act of *compassio* as he experiences the performance. 'What is involved is the back and forth movement of a reciprocal reflection through which the individual in an almost physical compassion is to also recognize and take on something else. . . .'[13]

I shall consider two audiences in the movement toward the creation of 'theatre events'. The primary audience is the production team or group, in whatever configuration, as they read texts and create texts, in rehearsal and performance. The secondary audience is the collec-

tive of individuals in the theatre, or equivalent space, which may well
be chasing the primary readings in hermeneutic circles, shaping what
they are chasing, including themselves. (Where does that leave me,
as a critic, in this race after meaning? Coming down the stretch I
glance over my shoulder only to discover that the finishing-post is in
the running too. It comes with the turf.)

Jauss sketches a history of the three modes of aesthetic pleasure:
poiesis, aesthesis, catharsis. In *poiesis*, the pleasure is in 'producing
the world as [one's] own work'; in *aesthesis* it is 'renewing one's
perception of outer and inner reality'. *Catharsis* names the pleasure
'which can change the listener's – and liberate the spectator's –
mind'.[14] In the modern era, Jauss writes, '*aesthesis* passes over into
poiesis', the perceptive into the productive mode. Herb Blau describes the structure of some of his group's performance work as 'a
[shifting] act of collective perception', and points to the 'idea of
watching as a mode of action and a generative force in performance.'
The only way to do research on the primary audience is, of course, in
practice, and I take Blau's tentative charting of his group's activity as
exemplary.[15] 'Cognizing seeing' and 'seeing recognition' – with special emphasis given to theatre's unique access to 'sensory cognition'
– is a point of focus. Jauss's history of aesthetic praxis needs to be
rethought specifically for theatre, for each new set of performance
circumstances, for each group as it were, and, as far as possible,
historically. The rehearsal procedure, acting-theory and ideology of
primary audiences need to be juxtaposed with the secondary audience's assumptions about these things, all related to social and cultural norms. Jauss credits Proust with a breakthrough – remembrance
as a new realm of art, allowing us also to credit those, such as
Baudelaire, before him whose aesthetic practice needed illumination
by the later, Proustian, practice. How does this relate to early twentieth-century theatre theory and practice – for example, concepts of
memory associated with Stanislavski? Brecht did a kind of charting
in the model books and theoretical essays. His clear philosophical
orientation helps, rather than hinders, *his* efforts. On this subject,
Blau also has something to say: 'Seeing what is there includes, in the
act of perceiving, being aware of the ideological moment within the
transforming system of history.'[16] (It might just be that 'ideology' is
a Chinese box even larger than 'reception', including rather than
being included by it.)

For Jauss the third mode of aesthetic pleasure, the *cathartic*, is
where 'subjective opens up toward intersubjective experience – in

the assent to a judgment demanded by the work, or in the identification with sketched and further-to-be defined norms of action'.[17] The
areas of studying the aesthetics of theatre in Jauss's terms could
perhaps profitably be isolated within groups, more or less consciously
defined ideologically. How does productive spectating function within
groups, variously defined – on class, gender, political or other lines?
This kind of selection would enhance the study of the socially forma-
tive function of aesthetic pleasure, as it interconnects with the perceptive and productive. One thinks of the idea of liberation from and
liberation for something in art (Jauss's terms) in connection with the
attraction of free play, improvisation and chance (not just psychic
accident) in all theatre – all, as I see it, attempts to short-circuit
perceived 'consciousness industries'. How might these apply to other,
social kinds of liberation?

It occurred to me that an example of the kind of work to be done
would be to describe and study the process whereby Athol Fugard,
together with John Kani and Winston Ntshona, devised the play *Sizwi
Bansi is Dead* in the mid 1970s.[18] This theatre work in an extreme
social situation, which in its beginnings even defied banal distinctions between professional and amateur, forces into focus some of the
variables which inhibit description or study: socialised behaviour,
mask, role, identity. What Fugard and the Serpent Players called
'play-making' in Port Elizabeth aimed at 'articulating a response to
the realities of the South African scene'.[19] The overt purpose would
enhance a study: where the deadly serious free play with the illusions
of one's identity and the identity of one's illusions comes up against
the facts of one's social existence. Kani and Ntshona's first performances in England were examples of 'heightened awareness' and were
awareness-inducing, if such things ever existed. (At least, that was
my perception – as we left the theatre, I and a South African friend of
mine overheard another white South African, apparently a business-
man, express his astonishment, and his envy, that a particular Johan-
nesburg company had managed to get a free plug by having its name
used in the play. At some basic level, a lot of this work is bound to
start as nothing more than superlative hearsay!)

The terms of perception, production and social efficacy in *Sizwe
Bansi* are not necessarily tied to the uniqueness of this case. Work by
any group exploring ideology, exploring the inner and outer mechanisms of the maintenance and reproduction of social power offers
fertile ground for study. Details of the rehearsal process are what is
needed, which then needs to be set against past rehearsal processes

and acting-theories. Jauss writes of 'the capacity to discover the truth' as being 'tied to what was experienced involuntarily, what remains inaccessible to the vagaries of the observing intelligence'.[20] Another reference to Proust. What is genuine improvisation if not involuntary memory on one's feet (*of* one's feet)? Which elements of improvisation, for instance, are foregrounded when the gender, class or other determinants are known? The only reception theory worth doing is based on this sort of praxis, on individual readings of our readings. One debate between reception theorists[21] is over the extent to which *Rezeptionsvorgaben* are operative in the reception of litera-ture. The debate could be mediated in the theatre laboratory. Do you see what you want to see, freely, or are you seeing what your material circumstances have programmed you to see? *Neither* of course, but where can we draw the line between them? One thinks of Brecht's comment on the actress playing a man and allowing us to realize 'that a lot of details which we usually think of as general human character-istics are typically masculine'.[22] Schechner writes of theatre as a place 'where new customs and their relation to old patterns can be played with, tested, understood'.[23] Heiner Müller has on several occasions referred to the ideas of theatre as a 'laboratory for the social imagination'.[24] Isolating the ideological field for the purpose of studying the 'primary audience' has its equivalent in the far more daunting project of assessing what exactly is perceived and produced and to what effect in the larger audience 'out there' – paying or non-paying, male or female, black or white, working-class or middle-class, and so on and so forth. Brecht had his ideas for experimenting with monolithic audiences to explore and fine-tune performances. At any point in the ideological spectrum one can do the same thing. To start with, in practice, one needs to isolate some of the variables and think about observed responses.

I have written about the aesthetic basis (specifically the use of chance and free play) of two very different German language play-wrights – Franz Xaver Kroetz and Peter Handke – in the context of the 1980 Federal elections in West Germany.[25] When the historical moment (this case) or social conditions (Serpent Players) force the perspective, observation and comparison can be more acute. Jauss's *poiesis–aesthesis–catharsis* formula could then be given some ground-ing for performers and audiences. It would at least work toward detailing a 'synchronic section', and be more than comparison for its own sake. In the Kroetz plays I looked at in 1980, the live running political debate (the sort of thing people actually watch in West

Germany) was a central 'prop', and a particular kind of chance factor – an example of 'world theatre' at work. The audience watched the actors watch live television; all responded to certain unpredictable statements, whose resonance was very much of the particular moment. It seems that Kroetz was using the modern movement of *aesthesis* into *poiesis* in a conscious way here. His ideological orientation makes it clear what kind of *catharsis* – affirmation in Jauss's terms – he had in mind. For Handke, the 'free play' would be an end in itself. He sets things up so you can make of it what you will. One would have to ask what kind of ideology is implicit in that.

When one transplants a work of art culturally, similar fields of speculation open up. Kroetz has had his work successfully transferred to the television medium, and over the years has had a successful reception in Germany (also on stage). Heiner Müller had, until recently, nothing like the exposure of Kroetz. His most recent texts, 'synthetic fragments', defy widespread dissemination by the media. (Anyway, he claimed that the most political part of West German programming received in the East was the advertising. What *could* it be the other way around?) Müller's laboratory for social fantasy seems consciously limited in size. One reads of his pleasure at a production of his *Mauser* by feminists in Texas. Perhaps the specifics of this sort of performance would be the first areas of research, followed by wider speculation on reception over (and under) other political walls. Two German artists directed Müller's *Hamletmachine* at the University of South Florida in Tampa, using local performers. One of *their* chief interests was the different audience responses for this kind of text in the United States and Germany. A striking difference, they said, was the American audience's apparent willingness to see parts of the text as comical – something which pleased them. In Munich, they said, no one laughed at the line 'A mother's womb is not a one-way street.'[26] I don't exactly know what can be made of a remark like that, but the enormous (and impossible?) task of charting response needs to begin with attention to such details. We *did* talk with a 'general public' later in the week. There are scripts which are more likely to raise fruitful questions. Perhaps the right script and the right cultural grafting is the beginning of a certain kind of research.

A very different kind of study, also rooted in practice, can proceed with a 'formalist' script. I did a production of Michael Kirby's 'structuralist' play *Photoanalysis*[27] for a gallery audience. In *The Art of Time* (1969) Kirby had sketched a theory of aesthetics which tried to account for the experience of what came to be known as 'The New

Acknowledgements

Two friends have been of particular help to me in the background work to both this book and the series: Clive Mendus, whose skill and virtuosity as a performer have been essential to my own understanding of what is possible in performance, and Bo Göranzon, whose passionate belief in the role of performance in the development of ideas has been a constant source of encouragement.

I am grateful to the University of East Anglia for allowing me study leave to complete work on this book. The Working Life Centre and the Royal Dramatic Theatre, Stockholm, whose dialogue seminar has been running now for three years, has set the agenda for the relationship between theatre and science: I am grateful to both for involving me so generously in their activities.

Anthea Iveson has done much of the word-processing, and her patience, cheerfulness and generosity make light of all the day's dull tasks.

J. H.

Notes on the Contributors

Denis Calandra is Professor of Theatre at the University of Southern Florida, Tampa, and an internationally known authority on and translator of modern German drama, notably the works of R. W. Fassbinder.

Heinz Fischer, author, playwright and leading international authority on Georg Büchner, lives in Munich. His study *Georg Büchner und Alexis Muston* was published in 1988 to critical acclaim.

Magnus Florin, director and author, is Dramaturge at the Royal Dramatic Theatre, Stockholm, where he has been assistant to Ingmar Bergman.

Anthony Gash is Lecturer in Drama and English at the University of East Anglia and has recently edited a special drama edition of *Word and Image*.

Bo Göranzon is a Research Director of the Working Life Centre, Stockholm, and Professor at the Royal Polytechnic. He trained as both a mathematician and a theatre director.

Julian Hilton, author, director and playwright, is Visiting Professor at the Technical University of Vienna. His book *Georg Büchner* was published in 1982.

Patrice Pavis is Professor of Drama at the University of Paris III and one of the world's leading exponents of semiotic theory as applied to theatre.

Per Sällström, physicist, is Secretary of the Committee for Future Oriented Research, Swedish Research Council. His book on notation, including theatre notation, will be published soon.

Elinor Shaffer, Reader in Comparative Literature at the University of East Anglia and Visiting Professor at Brown and Stanford Universities, United States, is editor of *Comparative Criticism* and has recently published a study of Samuel Butler as painter.

Theatre'. His suggestions about the perception-changing and by extension consciousness-changing aspects of art in what he referred to as 'situational aesthetics' and 'historical aesthetics' recall Jauss's earlier horizon theory.[28] So does the value attached to significant innovation in art. In *Photoanalysis*:

> The performance space is defined by three screens that face the audience. There is a lectern in front of the center screen and there are seats before the screens on the right and left. A different presentation unfolds on each of these screens as slide projections flash by and actors at each of the screens speak. The center screen is devoted to a lecture on the 'science of photoanalysis' – a hodgepodge of commonplaces that Kirby ironically parodies. On the left, a widow tells her story, recounting a tale about her husband Carl's suicide and her current friends along with worrisome suggestions here and there that Carl is not dead. On the right screen, another female persona, marked by colloquial diction, talks of her friendship with Amy, a native-born Cuban, whom the plot insinuates is involved in some convert, perhaps terrorist, political activity. In the story on the right, a character, suspiciously named Carlos, is assassinated. Throughout the play one speculates, detective-style, about the pros and cons of the possibility that Carlos *is* Carl, the alleged suicide on the left-hand screen.[29]

In the first production of the play, directed by Kirby, the acting was cool – 'minimalist', according to one spectator, who suggested this was a conscious choice, in order to point attention to the slides.[30] The work was produced under the aegis of the 'structuralist workshop', written by someone associated with formalist theatre, so the assumption that *Photoanalysis* was the kind of piece which semanticised form was a fair one. The simplicity of the script allows one to adjust performance elements and, with different kinds of secondary audiences, observe aspects of reception. I had the actresses take their lines as serious naturalistic monologues, and the emotional undercurrent led to something very different from minimalism. Is the productivity of the spectators different when the 'acting' is of a different kind? Does the greater degree of expressiveness in the acting increase the tendency of audiences to make narrative connections, to fill in gaps, even when the 'content' is purposely confounding? Do we see what we are in the habit of seeing, the pleasure deriving from the effort to connect, to conform to the habit? What would particular audiences make of the centrality of the male analyst, even if he is a fool? Is there significance in the 'radical' woman being on the right, or the left, depending on the perspective you take? Is it a mistake, a misreading, to focus on the (appearance of) content in the first place? It is not long before the questions raise the spectre of the fanatical Photoanalyst himself – analysis is confounded, along with content. Because the script seems to have been generated in an atmosphere of 'reception theory', however, this sort of empirical research could be of interest. I found a mix of responses to the play – some people irritated by the 'opacity', some delighted by the chance to piece together the 'story', a number amused at the joke at the expense of art and performance 'analysers'. (Incidentally, a few weeks ago I wrote to Kirby to ask what he had in mind for the performers. His answer says something about primary and secondary 'readings' in itself: 'I really wanted a very "method" production, although it did not work out that way.' The 'minimalism', apparently, was 'out there', in the limited capacity of the first performers, or in the critic's head as he sat in a small New York loft.)[31]

These suggestions for several kinds of preliminary studies, taking account of Jauss's main ideas, fall within the scope of his recent programme. What he said in an interview draws his own thinking in terms of art in general very close to what theatre practitioners have speculated on and practised for years. He is concerned with how 'spaces for play' can meaningfully be filled, how 'aesthetic education' (as he calls interaction with art) can make possible today, 'as he has already made possible in the secular tradition, man's putting his free play in opposition to the compulsions of work. Perhaps', he goes on, 'it will also reveal how work must once again be constituted in order to approach the freedom of play.'[32] Working hard at making (unalienated) play is a core activity in theatre. Maybe Jauss's aesthetic history can provide a lens to sharpen the critical focus on the activity itself.

NOTES

1. The best introduction to the subject of the aesthetics of reception in English is Robert C. Holub, *Reception Theory* (New York, 1984).
2. See Roman Jacobson, *Linguistics and Poetics* (1960), and Hans Robert Jauss, 'Literary History as a Challenge to Literary Theory', in Hans Robert Jauss (ed.), *Towards an Aesthetic of Reception* (Minneapolis, 1982).

3. See Hans Robert Jauss, *Aesthetic Experience and Literary Hermeneutics* (Minneapolis, 1982).

4. Patrice Pavis, 'Toward a Semiology of the *Mise-en-Scène?*', in *Languages of the Stage*, Performing Arts Journal Press (New York, 1982) p. 160.
   Pavis's terminology is useful: *mise-en-scène*, the interrelationship of the systems of performance, particularly the link between text and performance; *theatre event*, the totality of the unfolding production of the *mise-en-scène* and of its reception by the public, and the exchanges between the two; *performance text*, the *mise-en-scène* of a reading and any possible account of this reading by the spectator.

5. Pavis, 'Toward a Semiology of the Mise-en-Scène?', p. 90.

6. Holub, *Reception Theory*, p. 59.

7. Quoted from Jauss, *Reception*, p. xiv.

8. Quoted from Holub, *Reception Theory*, p. 154.

9. Quoted from Jauss, *Reception*, p. xxix.

10. Roland Barthes, *Pleasure of the Text*, quoted in Holub, *Reception Theory*, p. 154.

11. Jauss, *Aesthetic Experience*, p. 33.

12. Ibid., p. 101.

13. Ibid., p. 102.

14. Ibid., pp. 34–5.

15. Herbert Blau, *Take up the Bodies* (Urbana, Ill., 1982) p. 93. On p. 205, he describes this process further: 'What we formally arrive at has been approximated in an almost infinite series of substitutions over a long period of time within the closure of a finite ensemble. While actors replace each other at the same level of emotion – the glyphs of reflection as identical as dissimilar bodies can make them – the stress is on the collectively *shaped* perception.'

16. Ibid., p. 242.

17. Jauss, *Aesthetic Experience*, p. 35.

18. Fugard, Kani and Ntshona explicitly aimed at 'articulating a response to the realities of the South African Scene' (quoted from programme note, *Sizwi Bansi is Dead*, Royal Court Theatre). Where 'illusion' and 'identity' have a strong social basis, the problems of 'perception' quickly move beyond speculative aesthetics. The residue of their performance work contrasts sharply with Blau's.

19. Ibid.

20. Jauss, *Aesthetic Experience*, p. 33.

21. For a general discussion of this debate see Denis Calandra, *New German Dramatists* (London, 1983) *passim*.

22. Quoted in ibid., p. 76.

23. Quoted in ibid., p. 99.

24. Quoted in ibid., p. 138.

25. Ibid.

26. I served as dramaturge for the production of *Hamlet Machine*, attending to problematic details in translation as well as to a number of rehearsal/production questions. The directors were Kurt Bildstein and Georg Froscher (Freies Theater, Munich), who spent six weeks 'train-

ing' actors and mounting *Hamlet Machine* in the spring of 1984 at the University of South Florida. They had previously produced it in Munich in their warehouse headquarters (1981).

27. Michael Kirby, *Photoanalysis* (Seoul, Korea; available from *The Drama Review*, New York).

28. The première performance is described by Noel Carroll, 'The Mystery Plays of Michael Kirby', *The Drama Review*, 23, no. 3 (T83), Winter 1979, pp. 103–12.

29. Ibid., pp. 103–4.

30. Ibid., p. 110.

31. Correspondence with the author.

32. Quoted in Hans-Thies Lehmann, 'Das Ende der Macht auf dem Theater', *Theater Heute*, 23, no. 12 (1982) p. 24.

Chapter 3

Production and Reception in the Theatre

PATRICE PAVIS
Translated by Susan Melrose

There is nothing original in the observation that we can approach text
and performance both from the point of view of their production and
of their reception: we can study text sources, the literary context,
influence on the author, the refining of the *mise-en-scène* in the
rehearsal process,[1] the material conditions of performance, and so on.
Communication theory, applied somewhat mechanically to literary
works, has led to the imposition of the idea that art is a one-way
communication process between emitter and receiver (author/poet/
dramatist, on the one hand, and reader/spectator, and so on, on the
other), both of which sets of terms can be rapidly assimilated into the
economist's model of producer and consumer.[2]

At present, as a result of research into the aesthetics of reception,
it is the role of the receiver which we tend to stress. The 'role of the
reader',[3] 'the school for spectators',[4] 'the spectator's task'[5] – each of
these recent titles clearly indicates this change in perspective. Preoccupied as they are with the question of reception, the writers in
question would do well to recall the shortcomings of unilateral pro-
nouncements – such as we have seen in the area of the aesthetics of
production – and to re-establish the dialectic between production and
reception. Does not every option chosen contain within it its opposing principle? No production is ever achieved without the point of
view of the potential receiver being taken into account; and every act

of reception must acknowledge the production process. No creator of theatre would ever really risk writing a text or constructing a performance without taking the conditions of the public's receptivity into account. As for the way in which we receive the material of the performance and work on it, we cannot totally ignore, as at the very least a guiding principle, the textual and performance systems which organise the range of sign systems proposed by the producers.

What is clearly revealed in the notion of *dramaturgical analysis* is that a dialectical model, drawing as much on the aesthetics of production as on those of reception, is indispensable to theatrical theory.[6] Dramaturgical analysis (by the director) of the text to be staged, or (by the spectator) of the finished *mise-en-scène*, consists in fact of retrieving the system produced by the dramatic conception, and of constructing a system of oppositions on the basis of what is received by the reader or the contemporary spectator. Analysis of the work of the dramatist (of the text as read or of the performance as it is perceived) becomes a mediation, an articulation, between production and reception. But what we still have to make clear is how, within the work of the dramatist, three essential concepts organise the mediation between these two instances: (1) concretisation, (2) fictionalisation and (3) the textualisation of the text's ideology/ideologisation.

Production versus reception: opposing theories

Aesthetics of production and the primacy of the sign

If literary and theatre aesthetics have for a long time been focused on the production of the text, it is because this aspect of the exchange between the work and its reader appeared the most obvious and the most accessible to analysis. Interest centred in the first place on the aesthetic product as the result of work undertaken before the spectator's glance intrudes; it was easy to reckon up the contributions of – in the case of theatre – the author's intentions, the actor's declamation, the work of the stage craftsmen, of all those by whose efforts, according to Brecht, 'the *fable* is made explicit . . . the actors, the decorators, make-up and costume artists, musicians and choreographers',[7] who 'all contribute their art to this common enterprise, without abandoning their independence'.[8] For many theoreticians, this independence Brecht speaks of should not be maintained by the various collaborators in the creation of the *mise-en-scène*; they should not distance themselves from each other to draw the eye of the spectator to the process of production.

Instead, they should aspire to blend together, to efface themselves in one anonymous whole. This would result in an aesthetics proclaiming the autonomy of beauty and art, in which the work is isolated from its receiver without regard for whether it would be received by the public, or how. Walter Benjamin might declare that 'no reader makes a poem, no onlooker a painting, no listener a symphony', but the closing off of the work of art by an aesthetics solely concerned with production and couched in such dogmatic terms might have seemed total and liable to provoke strong reaction.

Early semiological practice corresponded quite naturally to this closing of the work on itself, where the work is considered as a *finished product*. This semiology, still overly influenced by distributionalist structuralism, applied solely to language: it sought minimal units and their functioning within the *text* being analysed; it was committed to the work-as-production as starting-point, and revealed a limited number of signs. The sign was the basic unit, tied to the encoding by the producers of the dramatic or performance text: this gives rise to a materialist quest after the minimal performance unit – that is, the minimal unit produced in time or space as the text was developed by its creators. *Mise-en-scène* was viewed as *mise-en-signes* (staging equals *sign*-ing, sign-making), determined solely by the creators of the performance. The ghost of intentionality in communication, and of the minimal unit, held thrall throughout Europe. By overlooking the fact that the system of meaningful production is developed not only by the 'creators' but also by those who receive it, this semiology was unable to explain the dynamism of sign systems, and the different rhythms of diverse meaning-systems. The result is a levelling of the meaningful performance systems, an absence of the dynamic hierarchy between them, and in particular the disqualification of the spectator, the sole person able to perceive both the hierarchy and the production of meaning.

What I want to do now is to propose a model, inspired by Mukarovsky and Adorno's scheme for the work of art, whose goal is merely to correct the non-dialectic character of any solely productive or solely receptive theory. Its task will be to solve the thorny question of the limits of the sign, or rather of the meaningful units and of the links between signifier and signified.

A panorama of theories in production and reception

In this scheme (see display on p. 29) the two aspects of communication are chopped up as abruptly and as artificially as they are in the various theoretical approaches whose balance it aims to restore. Here existing theoretical approaches are plotted according to a line of demarcation itself completely theoretical, with which the theoreticians might not readily agree; at any rate, despite their declarations of principle, they may – fortunately – not always observe the line of demarcation in their concrete analysis.

The schema should be read vertically, following the four main columns: (1) formalism; (2) sociology of content; (3) aesthetics of reception (*Rezeptionsästhetik*); (4) pragmatics. The opposition between 1–2 and 3–4 is established in accordance with an aspect of the work of art globally considered as sign.

In the case of the aesthetics of production, the sign is considered either:

1.   from the point of view of its signifier – the signifiers of the work are constituted by syntactic oppositions within a formal system of differences; or
2.   from the point of view of the link between signifier and signified (semantic relation) or between the global sign and its referent.

In the case of the aesthetics of reception, the sign is considered in its pragmatic relations with the user, the reader or the spectator;

3.   *Rezeptionsästhetik* observes what readings the *text* has made possible in different periods and for different publics.
4.   Pragmatics, the latest arrival among theories of reception, especially in the study of literary and artistic phenomena, gathers together several fields which partially interlock, such as speech acts (4a), theory of fiction (4b), rules of argumentation and conversation (4c), presupposition and implication, and thus a theory of discourse (4d).

Theory and potential

Without entering into the very complex debates aroused by each of

Aesthetics of production The model of the sign: signifier and signified		**Aesthetics of reception** Sign and receiver	
Syntactic dimension	Semantic dimension	Pragmatic dimension	
1. *Formalism*	2. *Sociology* *of content*	3. *Aesthetics* *of reception*	4. *Pragmatics*
(a) Research into specificity and 'formal' semiology		(a) Theory of readings and concretisations	(a) Theory of speech acts
	Concretisation *Fictionalisation*		(b) Theory of fiction
(b) Structuralism		(b) Theory of the activity of the receiver	(c) Laws
(c) Theory of text and of textual norms	*Theory of the text* *and of ideology*		(d) Discourse theory
		(c) Theory of social norms	

these four problem areas, what I propose to do is to specify each in its interrelationship, suggesting the outcome for the dramatic and/or performance *text*.

1(a)   Insistence on the signifier, and the syntactic dimension, has led to a formalist method which is limited to the functioning of the signs within a closed structure, favouring an immanent critique of the work and prohibiting the interpreter from looking beyond the closed system. The 'first semiology', which analyses the dramatic *text* or performance *text*, extends the work of the Russian formalists devoted to poetry, presupposing a theatricality which it laboriously attempts to restrict to a few specific criteria.

The failure of this approach could be foreseen, inasmuch as formalism rejected the role of historical phenomena in the reception of the text, then and now. Furthermore, the context of the Russian formalism of the 1920s (continuing up to the Prague Circle theses of 1929) is little known to the Western reader, because the relevant works by Medvedev,[9] Bakhtin and Volochinov[10] have only recently been translated into French, German and English.[11]

1(b)   The second branch of formalism has been much more productive, because occasionally it has permitted us to open the *text* to history[12] and even, in the Prague Circle's application of semiology, to suggest an integrating schema for the production of the work's signifiers and signifieds: reception tied to the changes of the *social context*.[13] This openness of Prague structuralism deserves to become one of the main bridges between production and reception, and in part is my inspiration here.

1(c)   One of the developments in linguistic and literary structuralism was text theory (or text grammar). *Textlinguistik* extends to the sentence, the utterance and discourse analytical principles taken from structural linguistics:

> In describing texts from minimal units to the principles of global organisation, from sound structures to major semantic characteristics, text theory offers the most systematic theoretical basis for structuralist poetics.[14]

The notions of textual norms, of laws, of coherence and of possible worlds are linked with the discovery of organising-principles of text.

Narratology applies to the establishment of the *fable*, and discourse analysis reveals how the dramatic text is distributed between actants[15] according to principles of coherence, which are not necessarily those applying to the distribution of the dramatic text amongst dramatic personae.

2   These three branches of formalist theory that I have outlined were constituted as a reaction to a sociology of content (based on the signified and on the links between the sign and its referent). This has accumulated a mass of knowledge about the social and psychological circumstances of literary production, which it none the less reduces to a pale reflection of the society or of the 'psyche' of the 'author'. So long as we lack a theory of text and of the mediation between ideology and text, this sociology will remain inadequate to describe the impact of society on textual form; the impasse is all the more unfortunate in that it blocks the path of a Marxist theory of literature which goes beyond the simple doctrine of the work as reflection of reality, beyond a conception of ideology as inextricably confused or false consciousness.

In perfect symmetry, empirical sociology (in the above scheme this is located near 3a) is every bit as limited. It inquires statistically into different publics, into reaction to stimuli, and impressions, but it is just as lacking in dialectics and tells us nothing about the work of art and its relationship with the act of reception. On these grounds, Adorno is perfectly justified in rejecting it as nothing more than 'enquiries into and classification of impact'.[16] An inquiry into the socio-professional make-up of the public hardly advances our understanding of the interaction between the work as sign and the receiver/producer of that sign. An investigation of this sort has nothing more to contribute on the production of content in the work, and still less on the mode of its reception in terms of its signifying structure.

3   On the side of reception, things currently appear highly volatile: it is only very recently that the bases for a global rebuttal of classic productivist aesthetics have appeared. Reactions have been very varied: Ingarden's phenomenology,[17] Gadamer's hermeneutics,[18] and in particular the *Rezeptionsästhetik* of the Konstanz School centred around Jauss[19] and Iser[20].

Rezeptionsästhetik draws on the aesthetic experience of the literary text by the reader, who needs to be aware of its relative historical position if he wishes to do more that understand the work solely as a fixed object, offering everyone at every moment the same meaning:

> A renewal of literary history obliges us to take our prejudices toward historical objectivism apart, and to base the traditional aesthetics of production and representation on an aesthetics of reception and of effects produced. Historicity of literature does not reside in a group of 'literary facts' established after the event, but in the effective experience of the literary work by its readers. This dialogical relationship is at the same time the most basic fact for literary history. Because the literary historian must first be a reader, before being able to understand and classify the work; in other words, before he can, in full awareness of his current position in the historical sequence of readers, establish his own evaluation.[21]

What we owe to *Rezeptionsästhetik* are invaluable hypotheses about different levels of reading, and especially about the history of produced effects in literary and extra-literary domains. For the theatre it is vital to understand how one play can produce different effects on the public. Here, once again, it must be emphasised – as this aesthetics often fails to do – that the sum of these different effects does not explain the text in question. Or else we have to show, as does Wolfgang Iser, that different effects and ways of receiving the same text depend equally on the disposition of production, which is a 'structure of appeal' of the text.[22] In the case of a Marivaux text, we should have to indicate that to a certain extent a guide to reception is inscribed in the text itself (for instance, in *Le Jeu*, where 'mérite vaut bien la naissance' ['worth is as good as birth']), though we may have to look to something other than this guide in order to grasp what to us is novel.

It is by introducing the notion of reading as concretisation, a concept borrowed from Ingarden[23] and Vodicka,[24] that the theory of reception and effects produced can be brought back to the process of production/reception of meaning on the basis of the circuit of signifier, social context and signified.

As for theories relating to the activity of the receiver (3b) and of social norms (3c), they flow from the general movement of aesthetics of reception, which involves the reader in the development of the fiction from the 'bundles' of information he possesses, according to the system of taboos and values which order his referential universe. These domains remain largely unexplored.

4 *Pragmatics* offers, in linguistics, 'not only a theoretical frame-work permitting us to treat subjects such as speech acts, argumentation, rules of conversation or of implication, but equally an original approach to problems traditionally considered to belong to semantics: reference, modality, presupposition, and so on'.[25] Transposed to the theatre, in particular to the analysis of dramatic discourse, pragmatics addresses itself to the *meaning* of words: who is talking to whom, to what end, what is left implicit, and so on. The results are directly of use in the analysis of dramatic texts and of the *mise-en-scène* considered as the demonstration (*mise-en-vue*) of a speech-act strategy which, as Anne Ubersfeld notes, is 'a quite specific situation of enunciation, in the theatre, in the sense that the fictional situation of enunciation is overlaid by – or underlaid by – a *stage* situation of enunciation'.[26]

Speech-act theory (**4a**) has become well established since Austin[27] and Searle[28] worked on communication and language games. Direct application to literature poses certain problems, as soon as we ponder on the success of the linguistic act within a fictional discourse, or attempt to verify whether the speech (in the theatre, of the text or of the stage) produces the illocutionary and perlocutionary effects intended by the enunciator. For one thing, unless we are careful this type of interrogation might lead us back to the normative 'intentional' view of literature: that is, where we attempt to determine what the author meant to say and how 'successfully' the stage transmits the text's 'desires'. On the other hand, we are not far here from the idea that the *mise-en-scène* of a dramatic text will only be a successful speech act if it scrupulously observes the directives of the text, to be played and received and understood as the author suggests: this conception is clearly tautological, equating 'success' in the theatre with what succeeds in the act of stage enunciation. Here the dramatic text becomes no more than 'a manual of instructions for use',[29] and the *mise-en-scène* is reduced to the quest for the most pedantically 'correct' way of staging the text.[30]

If pragmatics is justified in asking how the utterance succeeds or fails in producing an action on a receiver, it hardly seems useful to wonder whether or not such and such a poem or *mise-en-scène* similarly 'succeeds'. Succeeds in what? In producing the illusion? That is not an absolute and specific requirement either of theatre or of literature. In producing the right meaning? Who is to judge it right, and why should we wish to return to a dated philological concept which sees the correct interpretation as that which delivers up *the* sole and correct acceptable meaning? It is remarkable that speech-act theory, applied too swiftly to literature,[31] reactivates naïve notions we might have believed to be banished for good. This deviation towards an outdated view of literature as the author's intention which must be revealed comes, as L. Dolezel reveals in his 'Defense de la poétique structurale', from the revival of the notion of intentionality.[32]

Uses of pragmatics

Pragmatics defines the text according to the use made of it and the actions it accomplishes. Given the multiplicity of texts currently used in the theatre, pragmatics easily demonstrates that dramatic and performance *texts* lack specificity and thus structural definition (**4b**). Besides, theatre criticism, in refusing to acknowledge the coming of the *mise-en-scène* and of the semiological practices which accompany the passage from text to text uttered on stage, is limited to describing the dramatic genre with the aid of so-called universal textual criteria such as the presence of dialogue, the use of the first person by the speakers, conflicts and progression of the action, and so on. Structuralist poetics, derived from structuralism (**1b**) and text theory (**1c**), is no longer able to encompass and describe homogeneously the proliferation of forms and materials and practices used. As for the distinction that structuralist poetics seeks to make between dramatic literature and ordinary language, it is confronted by the methodological difficulty innate in the demonstration that any ordinary text can become dramatic once it is staged. The distinction between the two texts is not textual but pragmatic: one is fictional, the other is not. This confusion has been maintained because the renewal of theatre practice and aesthetics does not just occur at the level of textual modifications, but also through changes in the use made of the actor, the stage and the relationship with the audience. In this area, pragmatics is particularly suitable for grasping the modifications in stage utterance, and supplants a structuralist aesthetics drawing too heavily on text syntactics and semantics, and on the basic distinction of the formalists between ordinary and poetic language. But this advantage is not properly exploited; pragmatics introduces a criterion for distinguishing between the literary and the ordinary which is neither structural nor textual: that of fictionality.

In Searle and Pratt this criterion is reduced to that of receiver intentionality: if the receiver decides that the text is fictional, it is; if not, it is not. But it is abundantly clear that this dichotomy between the real and the fictional is a metaphysical leftover which does nothing to advance productive/receptive text theory. We find its trace in theatre theory in the eternal debate over realism and fantasy in the dramatic text. Frequently, what is more, this theory of fiction (**4b**) ignores the textual structure inscribed in the actions, emotions, characters and possible world manipulated by the fiction. They are not conceived as textual *constructs* by the theory of fiction, limited to a mimetic view of literature. The link between (**1c**), (**3b**) and (**4b**) has still to be established.

Speech act-theory applied to literature, especially as in Searle,[33] aims to explore the differences between fictional and serious utterances. But in the theatre is it really possible, within the dramatic or performance *text*, to split off the fictional from 'serious' references? The fact is that for the spectator/reader the reality effects, the verisimilitude, are the yeast in the dough of the fiction. This distinction between fictional and serious is not straightforward and definitive; it depends on the textual construction of the fiction, which is tied to the historicity of its production as well as of its reception.

Through all these difficulties facing speech-act theory in its attempt to approach the literary and/or fictional text, an old question of theatre practice reappears: where to locate the action. It is certainly not localised in the stage actions which accompany the text; and in the theatre, to quote the celebrated words of the Abbé of Aubignac (1657), 'to speak is to act'.[34] But it would be wrong to believe that the dramatic text produces acts on stage, losing itself in them, from the moment that it is staged: the text remains audible as a verbal structure in spite of the stage event with which its emission coincides.

The major objection we might make to speech-act theory, that of disguised intentionality, of an all-powerful author addressing himself to a perspicacious reader, should not blind us to the services rendered to action theory. The work of Oswald Ducrot[35] on presupposition and implication cannot be overlooked here. Ducrot outlines a theory of enunciation and of discourse (**4d**) which needs to be brought face to face with the theory of textual norms (**1c**) and social norms (**3c**).

In the concept of concretisation which follows, itself borrowed from Ingarden via Vodicka, and which will outline the notion of interpretation by one reader, or by one spectator, or by a given public, it is vital to avoid making it seem the 'correct' result of a pragmatic act commanding the sole 'good' reading of the text – as is the case in certain caricatural attempts inspired by pragmatics.[36] As long as pragmatics seeks out the conditions permitting an act of communication to succeed, it approaches an 'average' critique of text, abstracting historical norms of production and reception. Thus it is impossible to explain how and why the same text has, in the course of its history, known a dozen contradictory concretisations and 'successes'. If, however, we give up abstract and ahistoric criteria for universal success, if we establish a repertory of pertinent traits of dramatic structure, and of public expectation according to changes in historical conditions of reception, then these concretisations appear explicable, tied to a dialectic between the work considered as modifiable signifier/signified, and the *social context*. Controlled in this way by a knowledge of the historical reasons for reception, pragmatics and, in particular, speech-act theory, become fruitful in the analysis of successive concretisations. However, there is a danger that our patient speech-act theory will fail to survive so radical a historical treatment.

Forging links

What can we do, faced as we are with the four strong, solid and much-studied columns of this structure, whose symmetry is so unfortunately based on the opposition between production and reception? Our first reaction must be to re-establish contact between the two unjustly separated poles, to forge several links under the auspices of the three main questions aesthetics constantly poses.

(i)   How do we read a text given the influence of critical inquiry into its production and reception? What *global sign* ends up emerging from it here and now? *How is it concretised?*

(ii) How is the fiction constituted through the interlocking efforts of the textual programme and the reader? *How is it fictionalised?*

(iii) How can the text be linked with its context, how can traces of ideology be relocated, and how can we find the signs of textualisation in the ideology? *How is the text ideologised and how is the ideology textualised?*

These links remain extremely fragile, but they are at least conceivable.

(i)   Concretisation: formalism in its structuralist version (**1b**) and in its opposition to the theory of reflection (**2**) has been challenged since the investigation into levels of reading (**3a**); these are resolutely pragmatic in attitude, laying great stress on changes in the *social context* (**4, 3b, 3c**).

(ii) Fictionalisation: the theory of fiction (**4b**) is developed from a reflection on the conventions, conversation rules (**4c**) and discourse analysis (**4d**); obviously it is subject to the activity of the receiver (**3b**), but – and this must be demonstrated – in the latter's capacity to decipher or establish a theory of text (**1c**).

(iii) Textualising ideology and ideologising of text: this level encompasses the first two: textual norms (**1c**) and social norms are brought together in the context of the relationship of the text to ideological and discursive formation (**4d**).

What I shall be looking at here is the first of these three links.

There are two principles guiding our attempt at mediating between the four columns. First, we cannot pin our hopes on a middle ground, on a synthesis of all points of view, whether it is called communication[37] or desired communication or – quite the opposite – a complete lack of communicative contact between production and reception: a lack for which Adorno, via his negative dialectics, affords us the apparent metaphor. Only apparent, however, because the second principle is that of paying court to the paradox which sees the social in the form and the form already imprinted with the social; the work of art is characterised at one and the same time by meaningful autonomy and by social fact. Both Adorno and Mukarovsky formulate this proposal, but on the basis of quite different premises. Mukarovsky:

> The two semiological functions, communicative and autonomous, co-existing in the communicative arts, together constitute one of the dialectical antinomies essential to the evolution of these arts; their duality is manifested in the process of this evolution through constant oscillations in the relationship to reality.[38]

Adorno:

> In reality, it would be idealistic to merely localise the relationship of art and society in the structural problems of the society, as socially mediated. The ambiguous character of art, autonomy and

social fact, always manifests itself in dependency and intense conflict between the two spheres.[39]

Between the prophetic lines of a Mukarovsky extending Saussurean structuralism by opening it to individual speech and to history, and the aphorisms of an Adorno denying ideology the better to dominate it, we might hope to establish a certain continuity, and to pay homage to their thoughts by pushing them towards the beginnings of a semiology finally freed from its original formalism, towards a critical and social semiology, a socio-semiotics, if the expression does not seem too pleonastic. Such a quest joins another major current of recent critical theory: socio-criticism, that 'poetics of sensibility, inseparable from a reading of the ideological in its textual specificity'.[40]

Reception and concretisation

The circuit of concretisation

To fill what is only an artificially created gap between production and reception, what is needed is a model which does not fall between a formalism completely closed to the referent in its productive and receptive qualities, and a mimetism incapable of organising the text, said to represent the real, into units of meaning. The formalist model inspired by Saussure, limiting the analysis to the links between Sa and Se,[41] seems hardly able to fill the gap, because it is hardly able to resolve the question of the relationship of the work of art to the reality it produces or which receives it. This obstacle is no different from that confronting formalism in the 1920s, before a semiological theory of art as social fact appeared, offering the beginnings of a response.

As for Peirce's semiotics,[42] where a trinary model (representamen, object, interpretant) might seem to offer a way of approaching the referent, today it hardly appears able to demonstrate the mechanics of production/reception, since the referent, having no place in it, is unable to modify the work of art. Besides, the Peircean model is ill-equipped to establish an ideological theory, since it clearly distinguishes between science and art.

Mukarovsky's concept, propounded in 'Art as Semiological Fact' (1934), offers a good basis for describing the work of art's mode of signification, particularly in its relationship to what is vaguely described as 'the thing signified'. The work of art[43] is here defined as an autonomous sign:

Every work of art is an *autonomous* sign, comprising: 1. its status of 'thing-ness', functioning as a tangible symbol; 2. an aesthetic object, residing in the collective consciousness, and functioning as meaningful; 3. a relationship to the thing signified, a relationship aimed not at independent existence – since it is an autonomous sign – but the total context of social phenomena (science, philosophy, religion, politics, economics, and so on) of the given environment.[44]

This model, derived from the Saussurean model (Sa/Se), includes the relationship to the thing signified. It permits us to think of production–reception in terms of the following circuit (see diagram).

A large number of questions raised at different points in this circuit need to be answered.

1. The determination of the signifiers before the detour through social context: according to Lacan's thesis, the signifier represents the subject for another signifier. The signifier is not constructed by the perceiving subject (belonging to the SC) but imposes its order on the perceiving subject.

    The limits of the signifiers and their stability are hardly important at this point: all that matters is their ability to take shape when they impress themselves on the perceiving subject.

2. The signifier's passage to the social context is not direct, but takes place through three stages or levels of *text*: autotextual, intertextual and ideotextual. The units which make the passage between the three levels possible remain undetermined.

3. The social context of which Mukarovsky speaks will need to be structured; it is at the same time *produced* by the work, in its reference to a possible world, and formed by the conditions of reception *of* the work. It is either the context in which the producers of the text inscribe themselves, or the situation of reception in which the work is currently perceived.

    It is the receiver, finding himself in this social context (within which the artwork's referent finds its place), who dissects the work of art. It follows that the way the signifier is divided up is determined by a hypothesis as to its dimensions and as to its meaning and that its division is a function of its passage through the social context and of the hypotheses as to its signifieds. Concretely this means that the receiver proceeds simultaneously in two contradictory manners: (i) on the basis of a divi-

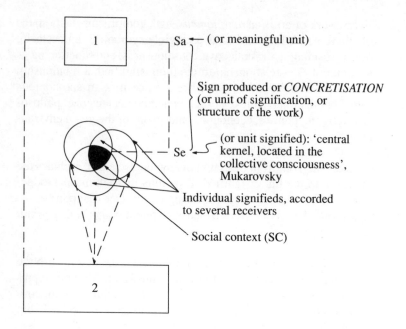

The circuit of concretisation

1. Perception of the artefact (its global 'thing-ness' – that is, the meaning-ful structure of the work): it is not necessary to divide it into definitive recurring minimal units.
2. Association between 'thing-ness' and the aesthetic object. This can only occur – this is where we need to make Mukarovsky's semiological theory clearer – through the intervention of the 'total context of social phenomena'.[45] In order to possess a signification 'residing in the collective consciousness', the signifier must first of all be brought face to face, by the receiver of the sign (reader or spectator), with the 'thing signi-fied'; this relationship passes through knowledge of the 'total context of social phenomena', which I shall hereafter refer to as social context or SC. At the end of this confrontation, according to a series of operations (fictionalisation, textual ideologisation/textualisation of ideology), the *work-as-thing* (or signifier) is associated with the aesthetic object (or signified) to produce the autonomous sign, which is thus the *concretisation* of the work-as-thing read or received in a given *social context*.

sion into signifiers, he looks for a possible signified: (ii) on the basis of signifieds induced through a particular interpretation, he seeks the confirmation of, or a trace of, these signifieds in the signifiers (SC→Se→Sa). Obviously such a division is not carried out independently of the work of art: this suggests signifiers linked to the social context (according to a formal theory of the ideological, to which I shall return) and more specifically to the ideology, which is not a collection of contents located 'above' and outside the work but, as we shall see, a semiotisation and codification of the referent in the form of discursive practice.

The attachment of the work's signifiers to ideology (or – virtually identical – the textualisation of ideology and its diffusion or disappearance in the form of the work) occurs thanks to this structured discursive referent. The movement back in the direction of signifier occurs then from the social context of the referent towards the signified of the artistic sign. The sign thus defined becomes the concretisation of the work, so that we can now associate a precise signified, corresponding to a certain reception undertaken by the reader/spectator located in the social context, with the signifier. The uniting of signified and signifier produces the concretisation. This second process, the inverse of the preceding one, will be described below, and will be called the ideologisation of the text. The difficulty here lies in describing (i) how the ideology is structured and textualised into discursive units which can penetrate (and transform themselves on 'entry' into) the literary or artistic text; and (ii) how the artistic text can provide a way of reading the social text, that is, the ideology already given substance, by establishing within it ideological units which are to be found, *mutatis mutandis*, in other social and literary texts.

4.   A 'central kernel belonging to the collective consciousness'[46] is produced through the intersection of different signifieds: it is formed by the element common to several signifieds, which, at a given moment in history, produces a concretisation, after which time the kernel is associated with a given signifier.

5.   What needs to be attached to the circuit of concretisation Sa→SC→Se *CONCRETISATION* is the quest, via the social context, after the way in which certain signifieds can imprint themselves upon the signifier, to affirm the hypothesis of the work structure in certain signifiers.

6. In the circuit Sa→SC→Se *CONCRETISATION* each term is variable:-

SC: literary and social norms, artistic traditions, the determination of ideological units or ideologemes;[47]

Sa: its dimensions, its divisions and associations, meaningful units and their means of combination;

Se: varies consequent upon the variation of Sa and SC.

As a result the concretisations of one text are innumerable, but they can none the less be explained by the variation of Sa and SC.

The origins of the notion of concretisation

At this point we have a sufficient basis for redefining the notion of concretisation, arising out of Ingarden's phenomenology, but already reworked in Mukarovsky and Vodicka's Prague structuralism.[48]

The interest of this model is that it explains simultaneously production and reception of the work, through a semiological circuit, and that it offers an explanation for the succession of different readings of one work, making plain the dynamism and the interaction of the Sa, SC and Se.

The phenomenological origins of this conception borrowed from Ingarden[49] explain the importance accorded to the reading-process and to the delineation of areas or zones of indeterminacy (*Unbestimmtheitsstellen*):

6. The work of art (like every literary work in general) must be brought face to face with its concretisations which are developed at the time of different readings of the work (possibly at the time of a theatrical representation of the work and of its being apprehended by the spectator).

7. Unlike its concretisations, the literal work is itself a schematic structure. This means that several of its strata, especially the stratum of represented realities, and that of ideas, contain 'zones of indeterminacy'. These are partly eliminated in the concretisation. The concretisation is thus still schematic but – so to speak less schematic than the work itself.[50]

To be sure, this concept of concretisation reveals a dynamic view of the work (that is, of the *text*), which only exists in its successive

readings; but it also implies that the series of concretisations constitutes some progress towards the completed reading of the text. It
implies equally that the sum of readings, by completing the 'schematic realities' and by filling in the 'zones of indeterminacy', will
exhaust the work's meaning. That meaning is thus assimilated to an
individual act of meaning-construction through the accumulation of
still-implicit information.

This theory depends on the individual act of reading, as though it
were a matter of waiting patiently for it to be sufficiently complete to
allow one to move on from the schema to the reality signified by the
text. It does not indicate how the blocking of the zones of indeterminacy occurs, because it lacks a historical perspective on the 'sweep-
ing' of the text (by the individual reader) as well as on the series of
modifications from one concretisation to another. Each reader produces a different concretisation from others': comparison is purely
individual. Integration of the historical dimension to this reading-
process goes back to the Prague Circle and in particular to Mukarovsky
and Vodicka: the text is no longer conceived as a naturally incom-
plete structure and thus able to be completed through closer and
tighter readings, or simply as a more and more systematic progression of the reader; its reading depends on the historical evolution of
the social context of its reception and of the series of historically
attested or possible concretisations.

So the text can be infinitely concretised and reactivated, but that
infinity is limited by the fact that the number of variations of social
context and the number of concretisations (Sa, Se) are limited. The
text is composed neither of a unique and correct signifying-structure
that a 'careful' reading will necessarily expose, nor of a limitless
series of amorphous potentialities that a game of chance might produce. The concretisation process makes the elements of the structure
dynamic, instead of passively drawing on a disorganised reserve of
possible meanings that the receiver will choose among depending on
personal tastes.

A study plan for a historical reading of concretisations of one text
and of the relationships between the work and the way it is received
is an immensely ambitious project, but it is at least theoretically
realisable if we approach it in this way. Vodicka sums it up in these
terms:

1.   Reconstitution of the literary norm prevailing and the sum of
      literary postulates of the era.
2.   Reconstitution of the literature of the era, i.e. of the sum of

works which are the subject of a living evaluation. Description of the hierarchy of literary values of an era.

3.   A study of the concretisations of literary works (contemporary and past) – that is, a study of the form at which we arrive on the basis of the study of a given era (particularly in the concretisation by the critic).

4.   A study of the area of the effect produced by a work in the literary and extra-literary domains.[51]

Concretisation, description and interpretation

What remains to be established is this: on what bases do concretisations *in the theatre* occur? We need to make a distinction here between: (1) representations we have seen, and (2) those communicated solely through the diverse forms of documentation which exist – critical reviews, reports of the *mise-en-scène*, work-notes of the dramatist or director, mechanical recordings (disc, film, videotape, etc.[52]). In the case of representations we have seen, the *mise-en-scène* is a first concretisation carried out by the director, on the basis of his reading of the work (if there is indeed a dramatic text imposing its fiction on the work). The spectator is in turn invited to concretise this first concretisation/reading of the text – that is, the *mise-en-scène*. In the case of representation we have not seen, we first need to reconstitute the system which was at the basis of the concretisation, with the aid of written or audio-visual documents which are the traces of and the memory of the representation. To do this we consider, compare and analyse the existing documents, with the object of grasping the basic structure that determines the concretisation.

Every description of a performance entails a theory of description: what meta-language should we use? What units should we choose? Why even bother to describe? Description is an intersemiotic transcription from one system (audio-visual in the case of the representation) into another (symbolic or iconic). This system of transcription is either an iconic or diagrammatic print-out, or a verbal transcription into the meta-language of a natural language. Each of these two modes of transcription presents advantages and disadvantages. The iconic print-out merely preserves the performance for the future observer, who will himself be obliged to do the work of description and concretisation. The diagrammatic print-out, using a system of notations based on arbitrary symbols, requires the encoding of the transcription according to a very precise system, but this becomes hard to read for anyone who has not mastered the code. In any case, it is finally read and verbalised by the receiver.

The temptation to be seduced by a heady thrill of a perfect system of notation or an absolute type of transcription is entirely understandable, but it is wrong-headed: better by far to attempt to explain the principles on which the performance text is constructed. How coherent is it? How might it have evolved? These are the sort of questions that need to be asked.

Description using a verbal meta-language is readily – and even almost necessarily – subject to a commentary which interprets and so writes a new text. But it is also the most precise, since language is a semiological system far more complex than colour-coding or movement diagrams.

So this description will be verbal and the concretisation of the dramatic or performance text will assume linguistic form as a matter of course. In its precision and its flexibility, language takes on the form of the object described and in particular it permits us to select the specific semiological principles of the *mise-en-scène*, to move directly on to the synthesis carried out by ourselves as spectators (or, in the case of a reconstitution of the performance on the basis of documentation, via the intermediary of the global system of the 'presumed' performance). Once this synthesis is complete, nothing could be easier than to graft detailed concrete elements onto the directing schema of the concretisation. Thus there is no need to commence with a globalising reconstitution of the *mise-en-scène*, such as a reduced model, or a systematic and exhaustive dissection of the whole representation.

Concretisation and interpretation

The notion of concretisation appears particularly useful as a tool in the interpretation of the text and the *mise-en-scène* of that text, especially where comparing a series of readings or *mise-en-scène*. However, we need to avoid reducing it, as do Ingarden and in part Vodicka, to the psychological responses of an individual face to face with a work of art, to a simple 'form in the consciousness of the perceiving subject',[53] because such a form does not exist without being 'externalised' in discourse, whether it be a commentary, a review or, in the case of the theatre, an actualised *mise-en-scène* received by a particular public. So we can see concretisation as a concept which can become an object in a discourse or in a document which itself can be verbalised. It tends to be the *mise-en-scène* but not that 'intended' by the director. It is the *mise-en-scène* as it is made concrete by the spectator, as a *discourse of the mise-en-scène*: such a discourse is a globalising and synthesising system reconstituted by the spectator, and offering some of the keys and of the options of the dramatic and stage work.

In this sense, the description of concretisation, though an indispensable step in the study of the meaning of dramatic or performance texts, is itself only the first stage in determining the *meaning* of the dramatic or performance text. Subsequently, the concretisation must itself be interpreted – that is, located in the historical context which explains how at such and such a moment it was received by such and such a public. So the determining and study of concretisations cannot abstract the history and/or the hermeneutic subject. Concretisation does not become explicit and *readable* until it is summed up in a discourse of the *mise-en-scène*, which itself can only be understood from the time when the product of the concretisation is received and understood by the public.

The study of concretisations of a work can be clearly distinguished from a mere résumé of the commentaries inspired by that work. Such a résumé is frequently inappropriate if we want coherently to reconstitute a concretisation, and by itself it does not tell us much about the motives for displacement of concretisations, or about the new relationship between Sa, SC and Se. Frequently it is useful to work out the readings and misunderstandings which mark the fate – or the fortune? – of a work; but this has more to do with the sociology of the cultural environment than with explaining the new meaningful structuring of the work (the specificity of the circuit Sa→SC→Se).

Comparing from our present perspective several concretisations of one work at different moments in history only gives at best an image of an era according to the social context; in no sense does it give us a core or a constant factor of the work which, according to Ingarden, would be its common or average meaning. Working on a series of concretisations established from commentaries or other critical texts is sociologically interesting but does not help in analysing or interpreting the given work.

Relating to each other the diverse pieces of information on a work contained in the text, newspapers, in letters and scholarly articles, and in the notebook of the *metteur-en-scène* is a preliminary to actually grasping the work in its *concretised* dimension. In the theatre, this inquiry into the concretisation of a dramatic text is facilitated by the fact that the *mise-en-scène* is itself a concretisation in process, on the basis of the concretisation arising from the *metteur-en-scène's* reading and dramatic analysis of the text (the stage concretisation). But, as Vodicka notes:

> Even for dramatic texts (as distinct from literature), we are in a no better position; certainly the *mise-en-scène* is then *the* concretisation, but, when it comes to knowing what the concretisation of a theatrical representation as a work of art means for the spectators, we can only find that out from indirect descriptions and information.[54]

As for currently concretised *mise-en-scène* which we can directly analyse, what is needed is, as already indicated, to describe the performance adequately, not to be satisfied with transcribing it into other symbolic systems. This 'reading in process' is illustrated by the body, the voice, the stage enunciation of the reading and the dramatic analysis. Once the spectator forms his own concretisation, it is *stricto sensu* a 'concretisation of a concretisation of a concretisation'. This series of interlocked interpretations does not necessarily lead to a confusion of levels, but it is indeed accompanied by a certain difficulty when it comes to separating (1) the reading of text (accomplished in the literal act of reading) from (2) the stage transposition carried out in the *mise-en-scène*, and (3) the links between this reading and its stage enunciation. Reading the *mise-en-scène* ('reading theatre' in Anne Ubersfeld's formula),[55] this involves (not necessarily all at once): (1) reading the dramatic text as played ('listening to the text', as this process is often called); (2) reading the performance text into which the dramatic text is inserted; and (3) reading the reading of the dramatic text undertaken by the theatre practitioners.

Indeterminacies

Filling them in

The theory of concretisation is rather vague on the processes which come into play in the production/reception of the *text*; it is limited to relating two series of changes: changes in aesthetic and social norms in the social context, and changes in the way signifiers are divided and combined. It is linked, particularly in the work of Ingarden, who invented the idea, to the identification of zones of indeterminacy (*Unbestimmtheitsstellen*) in the work. For Ingarden, what are in particular concretised are objective realities and not a new structure and a new relationship between signifier and social context. The objective realities are for him spaces which are not precisely located because of the essentially schematic quality of the text, which needs a reader to be 'filled' by a visualisation of represented realities:

> In different concretisations, the zones of indeterminacy are eliminated in the following way: in their place there appears a more precise or complete definition of the corresponding object, which consequently has, so to speak, to 'fill' them. But this 'filling' is not sufficiently determined by the diverse aspects of the object, and can thus, in principle, be different in different concretisations.[56]

Thus Ingarden suggests that it is a growing knowledge of the *object* (and so of the text's referent) which, in the individual act of reading, permits the reader progressively to 'fill' the indeterminate points. This accurately appreciates the importance of a knowledge of the referent in the process of construction of the fictional world. But where do we find the material to draw on to fill these points of indeterminacy and, above all, how do we locate them? According to Ingarden's understanding the text is only a matter of time, of method, almost of patience, the understanding and thus the concretisation being as it were programmed in the text. But is this not jumping the gun a little? Knowledge of the *object* – that is, of the referent – is not given outside the text; it is subject to variations in the ideological horizon, which is as mobile as the gaze turned upon it.

Far from being something undetermined, neutral, that we effortlessly complete, the zone of indeterminacy is a *place of interrogation*, a meeting-place between the text and its current reader, an institutionally ambiguous and polysemic zone. It is located in that zone in which the text does not say what it has to say – either because its discourse would be too obvious (but the trap of the obvious is well known) or because the ideology and the ideologeme mask the social contradiction the text speaks of without adopting a particular stance.

Localisation of zones of indeterminacy

Ideology chooses these zones of indeterminacy as principal focus points. Their list is not restricted, nor their positioning definitive. As Philippe Hamon rightly remarks:

> The ideological focus of the text is indicated as such to the reader by diverse foregrounding procedures; beside those of concentration and of embedding of the four mediation levels, alongside the procedure of quotation, they are indicated either by inflation, in the text's lexis, by the vocabulary of modalisation (believe, wish, can, know, must, have to) or by law.[57]

Certainly such focalisation almost inadvertently reveals ideology. But just as frequently ideology is revealed as more deviant, only appearing masked by the insignificant and the obvious. This is so in the case of the procedures of implication,[58] of juxtaposition, of two propositions without explicit conjunction, and of enthymeme.

By narrowly associating points of indeterminacy and ideological determination – contrary to Ingarden's suggestion – we bring in the model Sa→SC→Se without prejudicing the outcome of the operation and thus the points where the ideological and the fictional construction are inscribed.[59] So it would be wrong to decide immediately and irrevocably, on reading (concretising) the *text*, the location of these zones of indeterminacy and obviousness. That would mean fixing the literary work and transforming it into an object by treating it like a painting with areas of light and dark. In reality, the text is like quicksand where signals guiding reception, and others leaning towards indeterminacy, appear periodically on the surface: it is well known that in the theatre in particular, specific episodes of the fable or a specific verbal exchange will assume very different meanings according to the situation of enunciation. The text is both quicksand and an hour-glass: the reader can choose to clarify one area, and obscure another, by inverting the glass, and so on, *ad infinitum*. If indeed – as numerous theoreticians claim[60] – there are mechanisms which guide reception, we cannot localise and concretise them in a definitive way. So the notion of indeterminacy/determination is completely relative and dialectical: last told is most telling.

Guiding reception

Instead of speaking of (fixed) zones of indeterminacy it would be better to clarify the process of determining zones and non-zones and to describe how such a classification is carried out. The notion of guiding reception can initially seem to straddle the aesthetics of production and the aesthetics of reception. In fact, this guide is written into the text as a tangible means of eliciting good reception – which still does not prevent certain analysts, especially those inspired by pragmatics, from slipping into the language of 'psychological tools of the author' or of 'central organising text thematics', notions which semiologists rightly regard with suspicion. So this concept of a guide to reception will be used not as a phenomenon of intentionality, limited to explicit and classifiable areas, but as textual mechanism instituted in a particular reading strategy.

Just as uncertainty always vies with certainty in a text, a guide such as this is never completely satisfying or unequivocal, and what makes it readable does so at the price of the concomitant unreadableness of other zones. In short, the problem is that of recognition, in principle, of text guidance, of the literary and social norm which separates the known from the unknown, and that the reading will change consequent upon the evolution of concretisations. The text and its reader, through their knowledge of the norm, appeal to a 'cultural *déjà vu*' or preconstruct[61] which is immediately perceived or at least presupposed when the reader is directed towards ideology or to other texts. The norm is linked with the intertextual and ideological and so to the evolution of literary and theatrical conventions and to the evolution of social relationships. It ensures that the dialectical movement between a certain concretisation (Sa/Se) and the specific social context will occur; it depends on variations in the social content, variations which, in exchange, will cause the concretisations to vary. In the quest for the momentary concretisation of a work, it is important to choose the one which at that moment permits the dialectical encounter between the work as global signifier (*oeuvre = chose*, Sa) and the social context:

> It is a question not of recognising all possible concretisations with regard to the reader's intentionality, but of recognising only those which show how the structure of the work and the structure of literary norms linked with a given era meet.[62]

Knowledge of the norm permits this encounter; it guides the reader in the quest for what is readable in the text (concretisable in its indeterminate points) and unreadable (unconcretisable or open to too many possible concretisations). The readability of the text and the guide to its reading depend upon the reader's knowledge of the norm, as Hamon demonstrates:

Perhaps we could change our viewpoint and in particular unify the different approaches to the norms (either as something pre-existing, *a priori*, a psychological, linguistic or cultural given, exterior and anterior to the text; or as a specificity alternatively constructed and deconstructed by the text and interior to it) by replacing it by the notion of *readability*: something would be readable if it gave us the sensation of *déjà vu* (or already read, or already said, by the text or by the diffuse extra-textuality of the culture; the unreadable part of a text would be whatever was excluded from this *déjà vu*.[63]

So readability, which guides reception through recognition of zones of indeterminacy/determination, is only located through a process of guiding/anti-guiding which literally 'takes the reader for a walk' through the text, alternating familiar and 'wild' paths. In stage practice, the possible oscillation of fictional status between illusion and its absence, the miming of the real and the insistence on form and play, is added to this code of alternation.

Manipulation and ambiguity

The aesthetic and even ethical question of use and manipulation is posed when we are confronted by this manoeuvre of the performance and dramatic text. The reader, the director and equally the spectator must decide where the zones of uncertainty/certainty lie, how fixed they are and how appropriately they are identified. It is the function of hermeneutics and social praxis, rather than of text theory, to decide where ambiguity lies and whether it should be removed or preserved. The concept of interpretation and hermeneutic commitment cannot be eliminated under the pretext of an objective quest for concretisations and for a description of certain sign systems or semiological principles of the performance text. By way of example, a decision is required as to the fictional status of the text, or of the origin of an ambiguity: is it structurally written into the text or produced by a change in the social context which obscures the meaning of an episode in the fable? Is reception guidance only that which the text claims to say explicitly through certain meta-textual indicators, or is it in fact what it produces and causes to be implicitly understood?

Concretisation and interpretation control the zones of indeterminacy, shedding light on whatever makes the reading productive, what makes the fable pronounce the commentary sought from the outset. By exposing the verbal exchange and the situation of enunciation, each *mise-en-scène* takes up a position regarding the plotting of determinacies and ambiguities.

This management of ambiguities is a phenomenon tied to historical variation. At times we feel that, instead of exhausting the text by systematically eliminating its zones of uncertainty, it is more stimulating to *enrich* it by preserving them and multiplying the paths of interpretation: 'The more plural the text, the less it is written before I read it.'[64] Barthes's formulation in *S/Z* goes as far as possible in the direction of an ever-productive and open reading and of a systematic maintenance of ambiguities. The theory of concretisation leads to unavoidable questions about interpretation of the text, and its ideological and aesthetic ambiguity.

Ambiguity and interpretation

Maintaining and eliminating ambiguity

Ambiguity is the coincidence or undecidability (for the reader) of two or several possible signifieds for a single signifier (German clearly indicates the difference: 'ambiguity' is *Zweideutigkeit* where there are two signifieds, *Vieldeutigkeit* where there are several). Concretisation need not remove all ambiguities, some of them being structurally integral to the text and indispensable to its reception; besides, it produces in its own right new ambiguities when the social context changes and a new perspective is, as it were, injected into the structure of the work, to illuminate or veil an element of the work's structure. The reader, necessarily part of the social context, is himself able to manipulate the text's ambiguity, reducing or adding to it. By removing certain ambiguities he 'pragmatises'[65] it, making it more readily consumable and usable in his (or her) own pragmatic situation.

This type of ambiguity, essentially dependent on the reader's estimation, on his desire to explain or to believe, belongs to a hermeneutics of the work and its reading, and is much more difficult to manipulate and describe. The elimination of ambiguities, like the removal of zones of indeterminacy, is both desirable, to make the text comprehensible, and prejudicial to the interest shown in the text. It sometimes leads to a purely pragmatic view of the text, eliminating the fictional effects, the artistic flow and the polysemy. If the concretiser is keen to remove all ambiguities, the text quickly becomes unequivocal and redundant (which amounts to the same thing); it is in effect flattened to a single level of reading, losing its spice and with it its enigmatic quality, a value to which our current literary tradition is very much attached. It can also happen that in other times the reader is only satisfied with recognising what he already knows. In this respect Yuri Lotman divides 'all literary works (and works of art) into two categories which are typologically correlative although most often they are historically found in a causal relationship':[66]

> The first class is composed of artistic phenomena whose structure is given in advance, and where expectations are justified by the entire construction of the work. . . .
>
> Another class of structures will consist of systems whose code is not known to the audience in advance of the artistic perception.[67]

Ambiguity is consequently both a basic mechanism of all concretisations, and *a fortiori* of any interpretation which compares a series of concretisations, and an ideological concept subject to historical variation. Owing to the present nature of the social context, it is not always easy to differentiate between a textual mechanism and ideological concept. Thus it may happen that the reader, in those texts furthest removed from us temporally and culturally, cannot tell whether ambiguity is programmed by the text or produced by an approximate reading. This ambiguity as to ambiguities requires a radical intervention, and immediate, unthinking commitment, or, in the case of a more scientific reading, a painstaking examination of other texts of the same genre and the same period, a painstaking analysis of textual mechanisms. Any text, and in particular any text distant in time from our own perspective, simultaneously loses and gains meanings; the determining factor is the link between the losses and the gains and the historical moment of concretisation, the meeting between 'the structure of the work and the structure of the literary norms tied to history'[68] – that is, to the social context.

Ambiguity, even if it is not an anomaly but a constant and a condition of the text's existence, varies at the level of its ideological status according to textual structure and the social context. It is regarded as normal in both the fable and ironic discourse, but out of place in a recipe book or instructions for the use of household equipment or a resuscitator. The theory of modern art (in Adorno, for example) holds it in high esteem, even making it the specific criterion for art, fiction or literature; and in fact it appears more satisfying for the reader's spirit and creativity than the obviousness and repetitiveness of a text for current consumption. In short, apparent ambiguities which lie in wait for the reader considered sophisticated enough to detect them have to be distinguished from ambiguities structurally assimilated into the text.

Yet ambiguity and polysemy cannot be raised – again, this is a decision and an intervention of hermeneutics – to the level of an absolute, making the text an unlimited signifying-practice, instead of opting for a limited number of significations. Short of endlessly repeating that the text being analysed is ambiguous, polysemic and consequently inexhaustible and without any real meaning,[69] we must decide in talking about the text that for the moment it has a particular concretisation. In what follows I shall seek out certain ideologemes, which will allow us to bring together the structure of the work and the social context *sub specie contradictionis*. This is in step with sociological analysis, as conceived by J. Dubois:

> Perhaps sociological analysis will avoid accepting polysemy in all the implications attributed to it by a certain sort of semiology. In particular, it is not ready to take up the notion of the dispersal of meaning based on such anarchic productivity of the signifier. For sociological analysis, the links between the layers of meaning are not arbitrary or erratic; they retain an oriented or structured characteristic which can be revealed through analysis. Thus several of the works mentioned along the way, including Bakhtin's study and Macherey on Balzac, see contradiction, in one or another of its forms as the structuring model of the semantic field.[70]

A sociology of this sort can only be developed if the listing of ambiguities is followed by an analysis of their function, by semiological work performed within the text to the extent of ascribing the ambiguities to ideologemes and to conflicting contradictions, which are the amphibious notions of the literary text and of the social text (the textualised ideology).

Redundancies

Zones of indeterminacy and ambiguities come together, as soon as they are determined, with what might seem opposed to them: the redundancies of the sign – at least those which, in Michel Corvin's distinction, 'cannot be reduced to language and generate meaning'.[71]

Such redundancies suggest structures, they infuse the play with networks produced by various signifiers whose residue can doubtless be verbalised; but the word 'residue' tells us clearly enough that the essence is elsewhere, in the exchange from signifier to signifier whose homology asserts itself before the isotopy does so.[72]

Ambiguity does not disappear from repetition and redundancy: it merely stimulates a multiplication of the same signified without necessarily being reduced to a repetition of the same information. As long as the sign, or redundant sequence, remains in the fictional and semiotic universe, as long as it has no recourse to a pragmatic use of language and communication, redundancy only apparently harks back to information already known. It remains ambiguous as long as it is not subject to an immediate pragmatic intention (a 'pragmatic reinsertion').

Absence or over-fullness?

Zones of indeterminacy, ambiguities and redundancies: these constituent elements are for ever a part of the textual landscape, at every stage of production/reception. But what we need to know is whether their characteristic polyvalency reveals an absence or an over-fullness of meaning.

Steinmetz's critique of Barthes's theory of the polyvalent absence of meaning is particularly valuable here. In *Criticism and Truth* Barthes postulates that:

What will interest literary science will be the variations of meaning produced and, one might say, producible, by works: it will not interpret symbols but only their polyvalency; in short, its object will no longer be the full meanings of the work but, on the contrary, the absence of meaning that underpins them all.[73]

Steinmetz rightly wonders about this science of producible meanings, placing it in the framework of a history of concretisations, which, by way of reaction, define the absences of meaning, which cannot be concretised:

The expression 'producible meanings' suggests polyvalence in the sense of multiple receptions which coexist without excluding each other. But such polyvalence no longer needs scientific justification, since it is found in numerous historical reconstitutions of acts of reception. This polyvalence mentioned by Barthes is only pertinent when we know what it can be related to – that is, when we specify the unequivocal meaning to which polyvalence is grafted. That means the text, its polyvalence and 'its absences of meaning' must first be negatively determined, on the basis of given historical situations.[74]

If it is theoretically possible to list, for one text, the historical series of its concretisations and to sketch the territories of these concretisable structures, it is much less easy to compare this with areas not yet concretised. On the one hand, this is because the text is not a surface that history gradually fills in, showing any remaining blanks to be devoid of meaning. On the other hand, it is because the list of concretisations is never closed and empirical experience never completes the text: the text is never quantitative but a matter of combinations and of textual mechanisms. Now, contemporary theory is as it were fascinated by the void or by a spatial model of the literary work in which ideology is concealed in dark corners. Philippe Hamon noted this recently with regard to the notion of *absence*.

The zones of indeterminacy and ambiguities, which have demonstrated that they permit concretisation without ever exhausting the text to the point where it becomes transparent, are indispensable *presences*, rather than absences though which blows ideology. We shall see that they are most often the place of ideologemes or opposed discursive formations, the place of exchanges in which the text's subject is evacuated, inviting the receiver to compare the text with his extra-textual reality in terms of the social context of the text's production and the current reception of that text.

A history of concretisations

The emergence of new social discourses

If concretisation, in its successive phases of description, contextualisation and interpretation, has developed from the phenomenological concept it was in Ingarden to an ideological notion open to the changing influence of the *social context*, it still remains a delicate operation to define the 'given historical situations'[75] which mark the significant changes in concretisations. Their periodicity requires us to determine historical thresholds, which are sometimes ruptures in the literary and/or social norms, sometimes moments of continuity induced by the permanency of the social context and of reception. The analysis of new concretisations might draw on Foucault's method in the *Archaeology of Knowledge*,[76] by observing the emergence of certain utterances in the text through osmosis with adjacent discourses belonging to other texts with the same discursive formation.

In theatre practice, where the stranglehold of the director on the dramatic text is nowadays so obvious, it is easy to detect traces of present-day discourse, in particular from the human sciences, whose methodologies rub off on stage interpretation.

Concretisation and meta-textual commentary

The determining of concretisations is even less liable to escape contamination by dominant critical discourse when the text is, as so often, accompanied by a commentary generally containing the spontaneous reactions of a group or a school of criticism. Now, these spontaneous commentaries, however aberrant they may sometimes be, however tied to a very narrow context of reception, end up by encrusting the tissue of the text and transforming it, even becoming one with it or substituting themselves for it. What French reader does not have lodged in his mind the yellowing and adhesive image of cruel and gentle Racine, virtuous Corneille or delicate Marivaux? No text theory, productive and a *fortiori* receptive, can ignore these interferences and their role in the development and overtaking of concretisations.

We should delude ourselves if we attempted to recover the concretisation of the text at the period of its first creation and reception, and to consider it as *the* realisation against which those that follow have to be measured. Frequently first reactions only confer on the work an inadequate or banal concretisation (even if it is guaranteed by the author's approval) and it is in later concretisations that the work is fully discovered.

These undesirable commentaries are unintentionally welcomed by the *mise-en-scène*, more than by any other artistic practice. No matter that the performance is ephemeral: as soon as the curtain falls, the performance leaves in the minds of the audience and performers a trace which is all the more difficult to erase for the comparisons it evokes of other *mises-en-scène* in the same tradition. Staging always means making a reading public, taking up a position with regard to the interpretative tradition, displaying a commentary on the text and the tradition and thus suggesting, with concretisation in mind, a metatextual commentary. The specificity of this publication and this metatext is that nowhere can they be inspected or referred to as written texts, yet the *mise-en-scène* will continue to have an impact on future stagings of the same author or of the same play. Even if the director has not seen earlier productions, he will probably not escape this publication, which quickly transforms itself into a performance tradition. The intertextuality of *mises-en-scène* is all the stronger in that it seems to escape the fixity of the written form, conserving itself all the better by oral and gestural traditions: in the theatre, *verba manent*, *scripta volant* (words remain, writings fly away).

Intertextuality and stage concretisations

The contemporary requirement of originality at any price in a *mise-en-scène* obliges the director to run counter to the encrusted commentary in the dramatic text, to set his face against previous concretisations. The increasing frequency of stagings of a particular play leads the director to contradict ('counter-play') – despite himself and through a simple obsession with originality – the work of his colleagues. That explains the worn look that certain texts, too often concretised, assume in self-defence.

Evolution of concretisations

Having described as much as is possible the parameters and the variables of the concretisation circuit, text theory, to be fully persuasive, should indicate whether certain elements of the work's structure evolve more than others, at what rate and for what reasons. Even if we compare a huge number of concretisations, we remain unable to classify concretised elements according to criteria of conservation or transformation. All of them are liable to be radically transformed from one *mise-en-scène* or reading to another, and at all levels.

Differentiating between these levels is an operation which is already arbitrary, since it offers a particular point of view on the work, a horizontal or transversal dissection which is both a structuring and a hypothesis on the functioning of the text. Because of this I shall limit myself to venturing certain general observations.

Structural modifications

Surface structures such as the distribution of speeches, the number of characters, the complete version of the text performed, are apparently givens which remain constant from one concretisation to another. Formally speaking, it is often this which permits us to say that it is 'the same play'.

The fable, the action and the plot[77] are equally often considered as constant from one *mise-en-scène* to another. But the fable is frequently reconstituted to some degree, particularly in the case of a dramaturgical analysis which, like those of Brecht and his followers, proclaims from the outset that it is only interested in the text to the extent that it can recount a certain story, most frequently linked to the appreciation of the contemporary view on an event or action.

The characters, especially those representing marked social or individual types (roles) mostly keep their basic characteristics, but the time difference can be seen in the difficulty we have today in appreciating roles once immediately meaningful, such as those of braggart, buffoon and misanthropist. Comic devices and theatrical genres (tragedy, tragicomedy, melodrama, etc.) have stood the test of time rather well; but they are none the less dependent upon the values of the audience, on the knowledge of norms: ridiculous/not ridiculous, permitted/forbidden, and so on. What does vary profoundly is the ideological code of rules of behaviour and social practice, making it difficult to read motivations and mechanisms for guiding sympathy.

The most versatile elements (determining the mobility of all of the others) are indisputably the public and the theatrical institution: as recipients of the performance, they regulate its perception, ensuring feedback by acquiescing to meaning or refusing it, by picking up or ignoring cultural and political allusions, by creating distance from or proximity to the fiction:

The effect of an artistic performance on the spectator is not independent of the effect of the spectator on the artist. In the theatre, the public regulates the performance.[78]

By pushing to the extreme the theory of concretisations carried out in the last resort by the audience, it would be easy to show that each type of audience, and so each theatrical institution, *produces a different type of reception* of the same dramatist.

Guiding reception

Being just as relative in their capacity to transform themselves from one concretisation to another, the mechanisms for guiding reception in the theatre concern at least:

(1) *narrative guidance* – facilitated by the spectator's predilection for logic in the story-line, with ambiguous episodes and actants assimilated into the framework of the fable;
(2) *generic guidance* – which relies on the spectators' knowledge of the structural rules of the genre and confers a fictional status on the text;
(3) *ideological guidance* – which by a series of laws of accessibility[79] establishes a confrontation between the possible world of the fiction and the referential universe of the public.

The best example of this theory of accessibility comes from this passage of the *Letter to d'Alembert* by Jean-Jacques Rousseau:

> Any author who wants to depict foreign customs for us has nevertheless to take great care to adapt his piece to our own. Without this precaution, success is never possible.[80]

It follows that the evolution of concretisations can only be appreciated after the event, when the social context has shifted the relationship between signifier and signified. This shift cannot be foreseen, nor can it be ascribed to given elements of the structure of the work (of the signifier) which would be particularly unstable.

This disenchanted statement certainly limits our hope of predicting all producible meanings of the work, but it does not stop us from analysing every new concretisation as the surpassing of previous concretisations (and thus in an intertextual relationship with them); nor does it prevent us from describing the set of mechanisms which come into play in its emergence, in particular in the *stage enunciation* – that is, the concrete realisation of the dramatic concretisation reading in the stage concretisation, or *mise-en-scène*.

Stage enunciation

The director's concretisation, his reading of the text and undertaking of the dramaturgical analysis, is only at an end and only exists from that moment when it is concretised in the work on stage, with space, time, materials and the actors. This is what is called *stage enunciation*: the operation in time and space of all the stage and dramaturgical elements deemed useful to the production of meaning and to its reception by the public, who are thus, in a particular situation of reception.

Without going into detail about the Saussurean concepts of *langue* and *parole* (competence and performance), or the pair chosen by discourse analysis – *enoncé/enonciation* (utterance/uttering) – we need to remember that discourse, as an 'utterance considered from the point of view of the discursive mechanism conditioning it',[81] is individual, concrete usage situated in language. In the theatre this discourse is the concrete way in which the *mise-en-scène* organises in time and space (the stage) the fictional universe of the text (its characters, actions, representations of reality) by appealing to a series of enunciators: the actor (that is, his voice, intonation, phrasing), and equally the entire stage, in as much as it is anchored in the present time of the enunciation of all the stage materials. These enunciators constitute a concrete image of the situation of enunciation by proposing a hierarchy or, at the very least, an interdependency of sources of enunciation.

Curiously, linguistics of discourse and research into enunciation in written or visual texts are inspired by the theatrical model, which offers them a frame of reference which is much more than the bloodless metaphor of the world as a theatrical stage. Bakhtin and Volochinov, around sixty years ago, already conceived of the discourse as the staging of the word (*parole*):

> Discourse is in some sense the 'scenario' of a certain event. Living comprehension of the whole meaning of the discourse must *reproduce* this event of mutual relationships between interlocutors; it must 'play' them back and he who understands will take on the role of listener. But to assume that role he must also clearly understand the position of the other participants.[82]

Ducrot, in works which are more strictly linguistic and logical (and not specifically concerned with ideology), characterises the utterance in relation to enunciation as in some way specifying the role of its speakers and possible recipients, as ascribing to them, in the theatrical meaning of the term, certain roles.

So it is only just that the theory of *mise-en-scène* now calls on the model of discourse and enunciation to describe the way that *parole* is brought into play in the theatre. For Anne Ubersfeld the *mise-en-scène* must represent the place of the discourse: 'The proper object of theatrical practice is to constitute the place of discourse.'[83] And in a more recent text: 'What is revealed in theatre (with the help of language relationships which we know to be theatrically fictitious or fictional) is precisely the relationships of language, a miming of the conditions of human speech.'[84]

Not only do we have to determine who is speaking and who is addressed, but we also need to grasp how the *mise-en-scène*, as a global stage enunciation, is opened to and presented to the public, how it puts on show (and 'into hearing'), through time and space, enunciations that permit it to be received by the public.

Enunciation is equally clarified by the *attitude* of the speakers, confronted by their utterances. These attitudes (in the Brechtian sense of *Haltung* or the way in which one holds oneself and behaves when faced with a question) are not confined to the gestural enunciation of the actors; setting, diction and lighting are just as vocal on the relationship between the telling and the told.

To take just one example, the actor's diction immediately expresses an attitude towards the text and the character. Diction is situated at the intersection of the materially offered text and the intellectually interpreted text; it is the vocalisation and embodiment of the textual meaning and the actor is always the final spokesman for the instances that have produced the text, from its writing to its dramatic reading: 'The author's text', noted Jouvet, 'is a physical transposition for the actor. It ceases to be a literary text.'[85] 'The problem is to bring the phrase to life not through sentiments but by diction.'[86]

Just as enunciation always has the 'last word' over the *énoncé* in the sentence, so diction is a hermeneutic act imposing on the text its volume, its vocal colouring, its physicality, its modalisation – all responsible for its meaning. By impressing on the text a certain rhythm, a certain continuous or jerky unravelling, the actor presents events, constructs the fable, gives us an understanding of both the dramatic text and the meta-textual commentary on it. It is the blending of this enunciation peculiar to the actor (and through him to the *mise-en-scène*) and the dramatic text which provides the stage concretisation.

Thus there are two linguistic *texts*, and two ways of analysing them and establishing a semiology: the dramatic text studied on paper and amenable to a semiology of the text which borrows some of its methods from other text types; and the text uttered on stage, to which all possible meaning-systems attach themselves, based on the visual or acoustic image. As Jean Caune writes:

> The text will be regarded as a material that has been transformed by stage writing just as gesture, voice and space are. The actors' verbal expression is not the same, at the expressive level, as the written text. And it is not so much its substance that changes as its formal organisation. The verbalised text is introduced through a way of breathing, of gesturing, by an activity and in a space. It is only of worth through its position in the global form and the relationships it maintains with the other elements.[87]

It is precisely through relationships and interactions of different signifying-systems, and thus of their enunciation, that we can best define stage enunciation or *mise-en-scène*. Classic definitions of *mise-en-scène*, those attempting to go beyond the tautology which consists of defining it as the artistic activity of the director, see it as a harmonising of stage enunciations. Thus Coupeau:

> The design of dramatic action is the entirety of movements, gestures and attitudes, the accord between faces, voices and silences; it is the totality of the stage performance, emanating from a unique thought which conceives it, orders and harmonises it.[88]

Apart from overstressing the role of the director, this definition makes the *mise-en-scène* into a kind of *text* linked solely to its production; the spectator's role in the concretisation is not mentioned.

Concretisation and meta-text

The concretisation of the dramatic or performance text is only fully realised in the stage enunciation; the circuit of the signifier, perceived from and through the *social context*, re-emerges to become associated with a precise signified, the ultimate stage of concretisation. So long as the *social context* remains unstructured, the circuit remains schematic. In particular, the problem is to establish which texts the public and the director have available within the *social context* when the text is received for concretisation. Without constructing a theory of the ideological and discursive formations that structure the social context, I want to regroup in a final concept – that of the meta-textual – the full range of texts already known to the spectator and director, and used by them to read the text to be shown or read. Perhaps 'intertext' would be a more accurate term to use, but the meta-text is also located on the outer edge of and above the dramatic text to be interpreted, and so I shall retain this term.

If I might use a spatial image here, I would say that the concretisation is crystallised from within, through the intervention of the circuit described above, but that the meta-text is constituted by the range of texts situated *on the margin* of the dramatic and performance texts whose confrontation with the dramatic text produces the meaning of the *mise-en-scène*.

The ultimate confrontation is that between the directorial meta-text – that is, that of the director's *mise-en-scène* – and the spectatorial meta-text. These meta-texts are unlikely to coincide; indeed, it is the distance between them which gives rise to their exchange, each having its own solution for reading the text and uttering it, and for establishing a link between that text and the social context in which both are to be found. Between the two meta-texts there is, so to speak, an exchange of civilities, a dialectic, indeed a hermeneutic circle. The directorial meta-text only sets itself up as such when it is received and identified by the spectator; conversely, the director is not or should not be unaware of what meta-text his audience expects from the dramatic and performance text, and what readings that audience is capable of.

The result of this confrontation between the two meta-texts is the stage concretisation or performance text, the *mise-en-scène*. All traces of this encounter seem to be obliterated, especially since the concretised reading of the dramatic-analysis process and the concretisation of the *mise-en-scène* are intermingled in the final outcome: the performance text and its reception/concretisation by the spectator. The spectator no longer has before him a text (read or still to be read) and a stage uttering this text. The uttered text and the stage enunciation are enfolded in each other, and difficult to distinguish. The concretisation by the spectator succeeds the concretised reading and the stage concretisation, so that the reading of the dramatic text has already been, when received by the spectator, the subject of two transformations. We do not hear a staged text, but we see the *mise-en-scène* of this text, its stage enunciation and concretisation.

It is then our job (as the spectators or critics) to recompose the system of this *mise-en-scène*, what we define as the *discourse* of the *mise-en-scène*. However – and, dare I say, fortunately for our critical faculties – we can compare this discourse of the *mise-en-scène*, this directorial meta-text, with our own meta-text, in so far as we have some ideas on the insertion of the dramatic and performance text into the social context at the time of its creation, and especially on our own aesthetic and ideological situation in this social context. So we are in a position to criticise the stage concretisation of the dramatic text and its meta-text, particularly if we can note its incoherence, contradictions or weak productivity to locate the zones of indeterminacy and ambiguity.

Thus, if it is true that we always, as spectators, perceive in the *mise-en-scène* the embedded vision of the director reading the dramatic text, we remain no less able – in the case envisaged here of a *symbolic* dramatic *text* existing before the *mise-en-scène* – to separate the two perspectives: it is one thing to read the reading of a *mise-en-scène* with regard to a text, but is quite another – and an illusion – to believe that that reading exhausts the dramatic text. From the stage concretisation by the *mise-en-scène*, it is always our own concretisation as spectators located here and now in a given social context which is in the end right: this concretisation produced by us by bringing the reading by the *mise-en-scène* of the dramatic text face to face with our own reading of that text.

NOTES

1. One-way, because, according to certain theorists, the receiver cannot respond via the same channels used by the emitter. See, for example, G. Mounin, *Introduction à la sémiologie* (Paris, 1970). (Translator's note.)

2. Numerous studies inspired by information and communication theory reproduce the Saussurean schema in which the message circulates between A and B, between the brain, phonation organ of A, and then the ear and mind of B; and even Jakobson's schema of six functions of communication reproduces the dichotomy and separation between emitter and *destinataire*, 'emotive' and 'conative'. See F. de Saussure, *Cours de linguistique générale* (Paris, 1971) pp. 27–8; Roman

Jakobson, *Essais de linguistique générale* (Paris, 1963) pp. 214 and 220.
3. Umberto Eco, *The Role of the Reader* (Bloomington, Ind., 1980).
4. Anne Ubersfeld, *L'Ecole du spectateur* (Paris, 1981).
5. The title of a chapter from de Marini's *Semiotica des teatro*: *L'analisi testuale dello spectacolo* (Bompian, 1982) p. 179.
6. Patrice Pavis, *Dictionnaire du théâtre*: *termes et concepts de l'analyse théâtrale* (Paris, 1980) s.v. 'Dramaturgique'.
7. Bertolt Brecht, *Brecht on Theatre*, trs. John Willet (New York, 1964).
8. Walter Benjamin, 'Die Aufgabe des Übersetzers', *Illuminationen* (Frankfurt-am-Main, 1966). This sentence, quoted by Rainer Warning in his 'Rezeptionsaesthetik als literaturwissenschaftliche Pragmatik', in R. Warning (ed.), *Rezeptionsästhetik* (1975), is concerned with the reception of the art work, particularly in the age of its mechanical reproduction, but is not representative of Benjamin's aesthetics as a whole. For example, he (and Warning following him) rejects attempts to construct a theory of the effect produced by a work using the example of Adorno's aesthetic theory. There is a misunderstanding here, since what Adorno rejects is an empirical sociology founded on observation and classification of produced effects, not research into the processes of reception:

> We must not seek the links between art and society in the sphere of reception. This relationship precedes the latter, and is located in production. The interest of the social deciphering of art must look towards production instead of limiting itself to research and classification of impacts which most frequently and for social reasons, separate works of art from their objective social content!
>
> (T. W. Adorno, *Théorie esthétique* (Paris, 1974) p. 302)

9. P. Medvedev, 'Formal'nyi metod literaturovedenii', *Kritischeskoe vedenie v sotsiologicheskulu poetiki* (1928); in German, *Die formale Methode in der Literaturwissenschaft*, trs. and ed. H. Gluck (1976).
10. M. Bakhtin and N. Volochinov, *Le Marxisme et la philosophie du langage* (1929), trs. M. Yaguello (Paris, 1977).
11. On these questions see J. Peytard, 'Sur quelques relations de la linguistique à la sémiotique littéraire', *La Pensée*, no. 215 (Oct. 1980).
12. Most of Mukarovsky's articles have been translated into English in *Structure, Sign and Function*, trs. and ed. Burbank and Steiner (New Haven, Conn., 1978), and *The Word and Verbal Act*, trs. and ed. Burbank and Steiner (New Haven, Conn., 1977).
13. This term is defined later in the text: it signifies the total context of social phenomena.
14. L. Dolezel, 'In Defence of Structural Poetics', *Poetics*, no. 8 (1979) p. 522.
15. The term 'actant' is used here, as it is in A. Greimas, *Sémantique structurale* (Paris, 1966), and Anne Ubersfeld, *Lire le théâtre*, 4th edn (Paris, 1982), to refer to narratological functions such as desirer, helper, opposer, and so on. See also Souriau's *Deux cent mille situa-*

tions dramatiques (Paris, 1950). An actant is thus a *force*, but not necessarily a character in our understanding of the fable and the drama. (Translator's note.)

16. Adorno, *Théorie esthétique*, p. 302.
17. R. Ingarden, *Das literarische Kunstwerk* (1981) and *Vom Erkennen des literarischen Kunstwerks* (Tübingen, 1968). In French, see 'Les Fonctions du language au théâtre', *Poétique*, no. 8 (1971).
18. Hans-Georg Gadamer, *Truth and Method*, trs. and ed. Garret Barden and Gohr Cummings (New York, 1975).
19. Hans-Robert Jauss, *Literaturgeschichte als Provokation* (Frankfurt-am-Main, 1970).
20. Wolfgang Iser, *Der implizierte Leser* (Constanz, 1972), passim.
21. Jauss, *Literaturgeschichte als Provokation*, p. 171.
22. This is the title of Iser's opening chapter.
23. Ingarden, *Vom Erkennen des literarischen Kunstwerks*.
24. F. Vodicka, *Struktur der Entwicklung* (1975).
25. A. M. Diller and F. Recaniti, 'La Pragmatique', *Langue française*, no. 42 (May 1979) p. 3.
26. A. Ubersfeld, 'Pour une pragmatique du dialogue de théâtre', *Lire le théâtre*, p. 279.
27. J. Austin, *How to Do Things with Words* (London, 1962).
28. J. Searle, *Speech Acts* (Cambridge, 1969).
29. Without taking umbrage, Searle confirms, as is logical from his viewpoint, that literary criticism must locate the author's intentions:

> There used to be a school of literary critics who thought one should not consider the intention of the author when examining a work of fiction. Perhaps there is some level of intention at which this extraordinary view is plausible; perhaps one should not consider an author's ulterior motives when analysing his work, but at the most basic level it is absurd to suppose a critic can completely ignore the intentions of the author, since even so much as to identify a text is already to make a claim about the author's intentions. (Ibid., p. 109)

30. Title of a section in de Marini's book which presents this theory of usage, *Semiotica des teatro*, p. 48.
31. Thus in Pratt's *Toward a Speech-Act Theory of Literary Discourse* (Bloomington, Ind., 1977) we find sentences such as these: 'Richardson clearly intends us to regard Pamela's style as conforming to the appropriateness conditions for the speech exchange in which she is engaged', and 'Faulkner intends Benjy's discourse to contract with the way most people narrate' (p. 203). The same criterion of intentionality is employed by Searle, who, in response to Derrida and his article 'Signature/Event/Context', indicates that understanding the utterance consists in recognising the illocutionary intentions of the author and these intentions may be more or less perfectly realised by the words uttered (whether written or spoken) (J. Searle, 'A Reply to Derrida', *Glyph*, no. 1 (1977) p. 202).

In the same way, we sometimes find in directors and theatre theo-reticians the idea that a *mise-en-scène* only succeeds if the conditions of enunciation of the text, even those hidden in the text, be scrupulously observed. This is a resurgence, more or less conscious, of speech-act theory, for which language is a *serious* exchange about reality, furnishing the maximum of information on an indisputable reality. This is a long way from the case of fictional literary discourse, which does not pose questions relating to *successful* communication, to serious utterances, or to direct reference to reality. Everything in the literary or stage text is fictional, cut off from practical reference: what interest is there in separating, within the stage or literary texts, what is fictional/non-serious and what is real/serious?

32. Dolezel, in *Poetics*, no. 8 (1979) pp. 423–4.

33. Thus Searle, contrasting literature and fiction, writes, 'There is no trait or set of traits which all works of literature have in common and which would constitute the necessary and sufficient conditions for being a work of literature' (J. Searle, 'The Logical Status of Fictional Discourse', *Sens et expression*, p. 102).

34. For an interesting discussion and application of this maxim, see the theoretical text by the contemporary French playwright Michel Vinaver, 'Sur la pathologie de la relation acteur-metteur en scène', *L'Annuel du théâtre*, ed. J.-P. Sarrazac (Paris, 1982) pp. 131–3: 'From Aeschylus to Brecht, via Shakespeare, Racine and Chekhov, words are not the vehicle of ideas and feelings; they are the *means* by which the action progresses. They *are* the action.'

35. Oswald Ducrot's position is precisely given in 'Structuralisme, énonciation et Sémantique', *Poétique*, no. 33 (Feb. 1978). See equally Anne Ubersfeld's analysis 'Pour une pragmatique du dialogue de théâtre', *Lire le Théâtre*.

36. Pratt's book, one of the first on the question (see n. 31), should not distract us from other more convincing uses of speech-art theory. In 'How to Do Things with Austin and Searle: Speech-Act Theory and Literary Criticism', *Modern Language Notes*, no. 91 (1976), Stanley Fish discusses the contributions of speech-act theory to literary theory. See also Derrida's response to Searle, 'Mazes: Limited Inc.', *Glyph*, no. 2 (1977).

37. This is the name given to it by Jauss in his discussion with Grivel on aesthetic experience: 'You continually require me to formulate dialectical solutions wherever you have reduced a three-term system to a dichotomy. This was already the case with the production–reception dichotomy, which establishes in your work the circularity of the literary process; whereas I feel that production and reception need an intermediary, communication, and that on both the historical and theoretical levels the fruitfulness of the aesthetic experience can only be understood in terms of the trinity *Poiesis, Aesthesis, Catharsis*' ('Au sujet d'une nouvelle défense et illustration de l'expérience aesthetique', *Revue des sciences humaines*, 1, no. 177: 'L'effet de lecture', pp. 19–20).

38. J. Mukarovsky, 'L'art comme fait sémiologique', *Poétique*, no. 3 (1970) p. 392.

39. Adorno, *Théorie esthétique*, p. 304.
40. C. Duchet and F. Gaillard, 'Introduction to Socio-criticism', *Substance*, no. 15 (1976) p. 4.
41. The contractions 'Sa' and 'Se' are taken from the French 'significant' and 'signifié', and should be understood to mean, respectively, *signifier* and *signified* – that is, the two faces of the sign.
42. C. Peirce, *Collected Papers* (Cambridge, Mass., 1931–58). For a brief summary of application to the theatre, see K. Elam, *The Semiotics of Theatre and Drama* (London and New York, 1980). Elam refers in particular to Pavis's use of the trinary model, especially in *Problèmes de sémiologie théâtrale* (Quebec, 1976), which applies the icon, index and symbol to the stage sign, noting respectively relationships of resemblance, contiguity and convention between the stage and its referents. This application, initially promising, has subsequently been challenged, although it remains a useful *initial* stage in semiological analysis. (Translator's note.)
43. 'Work' and 'work of art' are used as Mukarovsky and numerous other authors use the terms, without pre-judging the value of this work, but in the sense of *text*. The same is true for the French term *pièce* play, used here exclusively to mean dramatic text.
44. Mukarovsky, in *Poétique*, no. 3 (1970) p. 391.
45. Ibid.
46. Ibid., p. 288.
47. The suffix '-eme', as in 'phoneme', 'morpheme' and 'sememe', means 'the minimal unit of (the element in question)', 'Ideologeme' is thus the minimal unit of ideology in the text. (Translator's Note.)
48. See n. 24.
49. Ingarden, *Von Erkennen des literarischen Kunstwerks*; extracts appear in Warning (ed.), *Rezeptionsästhetik*, pp. 42–70.
50. Ibid., p. 43.
51. F. Vodicka, 'Die Rezeptionsgeschichte literarischer Werke', ibid., p. 75.
52. On such questions of performance description see Patrice Pavis, 'Reflections on the Notation of Theatrical Performance', *Languages of the Stage: Essays in the Semiology of the Theatre* (1982).
53. Vodicka, in Warning (ed.), *Rezeptionsästhetik*, p. 80.
54. F. Vodicka, 'Die Konkretisation des literarischen Werkes', in Warning (ed.), *Rezeptionsästhetik*, p. 92.
55. Ubersfeld, *Lire le Théâtre*.
56. Ingarden, in Warning (ed.), *Rezeptionsästhetik*, p. 43.
57. Philippe Hamon, 'Texte et idéologie: Pour une poetique de la norme', *Poétique*, no. 49 (Feb. 1982) p. 123.
58. C. Kebrat-Orecchioni, *Comprendre l'implicite*, University of Urbino. Working papers 110–11 (Jan.–Feb. 1982).
59. This quest for zones of indeterminacy with a view to concretisation is apparently not to be associated with the concept of *absence*, which to Hamon seems to act as a key concept in the theoretical writings on the relationships between text and ideology. And this same concept of absence (of 'lacunae', of 'zero degree', of 'gaps' or 'unsaid', 'implicit' or 'blanks') seems to have been promoted to the rank of funda-

mental, multidisciplinary and ecumenical concept *par excellence*, ex-
plicative passport for all analyses and a universal methodology for all
meta-languages, opening all the textual locks. Then follows an im-
pressive list of quotations in which silence rivals the implicit, ellipsis,
ignorance, and so on.

What Hamon is referring to here is the zone which ideology can fill,
which is not, as in our case, the zone which assumes a concrete
meaning for the constitution of the general meaning of the text or of
the representation at a given moment and in a given social context.
The zone filled in the process of concretisation is not, or, at least, not
necessarily, the sign of an ideological unsaid (*non-dit*) which would
explain everything by its absence.

60. Thus G. Grimm, in his *Rezeptionsgeschichte* (1977), speaks of signals
     in the work guiding various receptions and concretisations: 'One
     might suppose, at least as a working hypothesis, that the parts which
     intersect in the different documents of reception refer to signals which
     have an ambiguous textual meaning and that the divergent parts of
     reception refer to ambiguous textual signals.' For R. Fieguth, drama
     always contains an implicit receiver, addressed by the text – the most
     obvious and extreme example being that of the *raisonneur* in a classi-
     cal play: 'To sum up, we might say that the receiver of the drama tries
     unceasingly and without so desiring to analyse all the words of the
     various units of dialogue, to determine whether they should be attrib-
     uted with (a) the function of the author's argument, (b) the function of
     the mode of good reception' (Conference on Semiotics at Regensburg,
     no. 1979, roneoed text, p. 6).

     In its most extreme form, this guiding of the reader can be found in
     Iser's work. The titles of his books offer a veritable study programme:
     *The Act of Reading, The Implied Reader, The Naming Structure of
     Texts*. The linguistic signs of the text or its structures find themselves
     completed in the fact that they can initiate acts, in the course of which
     the translation of the text takes place in the reader's consciousness.
     This explanation seems more appropriate to a psychological study of
     phenomena of the imaginary than to a theory of text.

61. Preconstructs are units of discourse which are gathered as they are in
     the text in the form of presupposition, implication or non-verified
     proposition.

62. Vodicka, in Warning (ed.), *Rezeptionsästhetik*, p. 99.

63. Philippe Hamon, 'Sur les notions de norme et de lisibilité en
     linguistique', *Littérature*, no. 14 (1974) p. 120.

64. Roland Barthes, *S/Z* (Paris, 1970) p. 16.

65. Thus H. Steinmetz in his 'Réception et interprétation', in K. Varga
     (ed.), *Théorie de la Littérature* (Paris, 1981) p. 202.

66. Yuri Lotman, 'Le "hors-texte": Les liaisons extratextuelles de l'oeuvre
     poétique', *Change*, no. 6 (1970) p. 76.

67. Ibid., pp. 76 and 80.

68. Vodicka, in Warning (ed.), *Rezeptionsästhetik*, p. 90.

69. For example Zima when he writes, 'As polysemic signifier, the text is
     an enigma whose sociological interpretation cannot bring an end to

the enigma' (*Pour une sociologie du texte littéraire* (Paris, 1978) p. 132; text cited in J. Dubois, 'Sociologie des textes littéraires', *La Pensée*, no. 215 (Oct. 1980) p. 93).

70. Ibid.
71. Michel Corvin, 'La rédondance du signe dans le fonctionnement théâtral', *Degrés*, no. 13 (Spring 1978) p. 22.
72. Steinmetz in Varga (ed.), *Théorie de la Littérature*, p. 201.
73. Roland Barthes, *Critique et verité* (Paris, 1968) p. 57.
74. Steinmetz, in Varga (ed.), *Théorie de la Littérature*, p. 201.
75. Ibid., p. 207.
76. Michel Foucault, *The Archaeology of Knowledge* (London, 1974).
77. On these and other topics mentioned in this section see my *Dictionnaire du théâtre*.
78. Brecht, *Brecht on Theatre*, p. 266.
79. On the theory of accessibility from one world to another, see N. Rescher, *A Theory of Possibility* (Pittsburgh, 1975).
80. Jean-Jacques Rousseau, *Lettres à M. d'Alembert sur son article* (Geneva, 1758) pp. 70–1.
81. L. Guespin, 'Problématique des travaux sur le discours politique', *Langages* (Sep. 1971) p. 10.
82. N. Volochinov, 'Slovo v zhizni i slovo v poezii' ('Discourse in Life and Discourse in Poetry'), *Zvezda*, no. 6 (1926) p. 257.
83. Anne Ubersfeld, 'Le lieu du discours', *Practiques*, nos 15–6 (July 1977) p. 13.
84. Ubersfeld, *Lire le théâtre*, p. 290.
85. Louis Jouvet, *Le Comédien désincarné* (Paris, 1954) p. 153.
86. Louis Jouvet, *Tragédie classique et théâtrale du XIXe siècle* (Paris, 1968) p. 257.
87. Jean Caune, *La Dramatisation* (Louvain, 1981) p. 234.
88. J. Coupeau, 'Un essai de rénovation dramatique', *Nouvelle Revue Française*, Sep. 1913; reprinted in *Appels*, I (Paris, 1974) pp. 29–30.

Chapter 4

Audience: Osiris, Catharsis and the Feast of Fools

HEINZ FISCHER

I

Arctic silence extends to the horizon. Howling storms announce the onslaught of winter. The Eskimos in northern Canada gather and divide 'into two parties called respectively the ptarmigans and the ducks, the ptarmigans comprising all persons born in winter, and the ducks all persons born in summer. A long rope of seal-skin is then stretched out, and each party laying hold of one end of it seeks by tugging with might and main to drag the other party to its side.'[1]

No question who wins. Sir James Frazer describes this contest as a magical ceremony with the avowed intention of ensuring the victory of *summer* over *winter*,[2] a widely practised battle of the seasons, which, notes Frazer with a frown, 'in Europe has long degenerated into a mere dramatic performance'.

In Omaha, the sun glares from the sky. No cloud has been seen for weeks. The earth is parched, the corn wilting and withering. A large vessel is filled with water by members of the sacred Buffalo society. The men dance around it, drink from the water and spit on the ground. Then the water is poured out on the parched earth and the men drink it up, their faces covered with mud. 'Lastly, they squirt the water into the air, making a fine mist. This saves the corn.'[3]

Imitative magic, based on the principle like produces like: 'primitive' man strongly believed (in some parts of the world, still believes) in an intimate relation between sexual intercourse of a (virile) man and a (fertile) woman and the fertility of the fields and fruit-bearing trees which witness their 'holy union' (*hieros gamos*). This belief became seminal to numerous rites, some of which developed into forms of drama.

It is well-documented that every year, to ensure that the Nile flooded and fertilised the fields as usual, the pharaoh of Egypt had intercourse with his queen on a boat anchored in midstream. A direct affinity exists between the rites of this holy union and the Dionysian Bacchanalia (out of which tragedy and comedy grew), the *Fastnachtsspiel* (Shrovetide play), the *commedia dell'arte* and carnival processions. I have recently witnessed a carnival procession at Rottweil in Swabia, seat of a Catholic bishop, in which a group of young men marched through the town carrying an enormous bed. When they spotted a pretty girl in the crowd, they dragged her onto the bed and performed mock intercourse with her, in full view of all the spectators. The performance was made by the interaction of a representative of the audience with the actors.

We may, then, view the function of the audience in this ritual context as one party to a 'holy union' – the performance – with the actors: what once was performed to nature as 'audience', to awaken its reproductive forces, has gradually undergone a metamorphosis; now the audience itself assumes the role of 'nature', in a performance event equivalent to an act of copulation – the performance itself being, by implication, the off-spring of their intercourse. But the sexual dimension of an audience's function is not the only one. Part of the function of carnival rites (and many others from which theatre grew) is the public expulsion of winter by spring with whips, rattles, bells and loud bangs, driving out the demons of death and decay. This general theme of the expulsion of winter opens out the moral dimension of the audience's role, that of participating in, and affirming by its attendance, the act of ritual expulsion of evil.

Both principles, the notion of death and decay being overcome and that of evil being driven out, meet in the myths of death and resurrection common to many classic performance rites. The Egyptians mourned the violent death of Osiris and rejoiced in the spring at his resurrection through the love of Isis. Osiris was cut to pieces by an evil brother, Set, but his limbs were buried in the fields to ensure their fertility. Isis gained victory over Osiris's brother by collecting and piecing the parts of Osiris's body together, and Osiris came back to

life. In ancient Egypt this dramatic rite of death and rebirth was
staged with the dead god portrayed as a mummy slowly rising higher
and higher from his bier until he stood erect, engulfed by the wings
of loving Isis while an actor held up an *ankh* (a cross with a loop at
the top), the Egyptian symbol of life.

Another of the gods who represented nature and rebirth ('a god of
many names, but of essentially one nature') was Dionysus, wor-
shipped in ancient Greece. His devotees gathered together dancing,
'dressed in animal skins, wearing masks and accompanied by drums'.[4]
In ecstatic orgies, the god in form of a bull or a male goat was torn to
pieces and the flesh of the sacrificed animal 'eaten raw as a sacra-
ment'.[5] The god's flesh was believed to convey 'the quickening
influence of the god of vegetation',[6] and women who wished to be
fruitful were the most fervent followers of Dionysus.

Gradually, from Dionysus worship grew the whole body of ancient
Greek theatre. First, in ritual chant a protagonist (first actor) emerged
from the celebrating chorus; to him, in dramatic contests held at the
great Dionysian in Athens, Aeschylus added a second and Sophocles
a third actor. Takis Muzenidis, who has staged most of the 33 ancient
Greek plays that have survived, comments: 'Ancient Greek drama is
intimately related to hundreds of years of social and religious change,
and moves from the simplest magical rite to a perfect form of art,
concerned with what we still recognise to be eternal values.'[7] Society
– the audience – played a part in the plays development and legiti-
mates their themes as eternal by continuing to attend performances of
them.

The special nature of theatre performance in Athens needs to be
stressed: theatres were not open all the year round and did not operate
on a commercial basis, but were opened for special occasions, notably the Great Dionysia at the end of March.[8] This was the most
significant of the festivals and the best attended. A statue of Dionysus
was set up in the middle of the theatre by a procession of armed
youths; another procession of men and women, in festival dress and
covered with garlands, followed bearing offerings: 'Phalli were sent
by Athenian colonies.'[9] Athenian citizens did not simply have a right
to attend; attendance was considered a duty to the *polis*, the state. The
theatre was large enough to accommodate every citizen, and going to
the theatre became a practical expression of community and common
identity. It was also an event on which vast sums were spent: the
Spartans accused the Athenians of spending more money on theatre
than on war.

The festival took the form of a dramatic competition, with a series of plays performed each day. The audience were 'passionately interested' and made no attempt to hide their feelings, being acutely mindful of their 'duty to the gods' to be critically and emotionally engaged. Critical Athenian spectators are known to have drummed their heels on their seats to show their disapproval, and Aeschylus had to run for his life when indignant spectators rose and pelted him with stones: they thought that in one play he had betrayed the mysteries of Eleusis – secrets that should only be divulged to a handful of initiates.

It was a risky job writing for an Athenian audience with such high moral and aesthetic standards and accustomed to theatre dealing in the profoundest aspects of life – growth and decay, laughter and grief, meaning and nonsense. Members of the audience would express appreciation of a fine play by murmuring good lines along with the actors and learning them by heart. Play-going became a pastime as popular as attendance at football matches in many modern countries. Even today in parts of rural Greece you can see whole families travelling to performances, often covering long distances on foot. When they arrive they take out their provisions – bread, cheese and olives – and picnic, eagerly awaiting the start of the play.[10]

Whatever the expectations of the ancient Athenian audience, it developed a consciousness of specific genres (tragedy, comedy, satyr play) in performance. This involved a definition of terms – 'tragedy', for example, originally a song sung when a goat was sacrificed. The same audience developed a consciousness of the distinctiveness of actors and performers. In rite there had simply been a group of concelebrants. Aware of this, Aristotle attempted to codify the audience's responses in terms of terror (*phobos*), pity (*eleos*) and purging (*katharsis*). Wishing to separate tragedy from rite, he suppressed the ritual element of the expulsion of winter and assurance of new life in his theory of the reception of tragedy by an audience. He focused instead on the issue of artistic imitation, and saw aesthetic pleasure as deriving from the natural urge to imitate, observable in all children. The enjoyment of imitation, whether of an animal, a person or an action, was the basis of the audience's engagement with performance. Generalising further, he saw 'terror' as terror of death and decay, 'pity' as pity of the victim of circumstances, and 'catharsis' as the purging of pity and terror – corresponding to the ritual victory over life-stifling forces. For Aristotle, there is catharsis in any good tragedy, as there is in any rite of winter a rite of spring.

II

The emergence of Christianity as the dominant ideology of the Western world meant that the role of the theatre audience itself became condemned, since theatre as a whole was held to be sinful. Theatre was equated with venal pleasure, sensuous enjoyment and the affirmation of life on earth, all of which were at odds with the aesthetic spirit of early Christian thought. The first sign of change came around 915, when, it appears, a monk at St Gall, Tuitilo, added a short exchange of questions and answers to the Easter liturgy. This addition was sung by clerics 'impersonating' the angels at Christ's tomb and the three Marys looking for the body of Christ. It dramatises the situation of the three Marys, puzzled at the empty grave and the angels who confront them. '*Quem quaeritis?*' ('Whom do you seek?'), the angels ask. The Marys reply, '*Jesum crucifixum*' ('The crucified Jesus'), but learn, '*Non est hic*' ('He is not here').

This has long been interpreted as the rebirth, out of the Church, of European theatre, the germ of the Easter passion-plays, the Mystery cycles and morality interludes. Scholars have attempted to explain why Tuitilo's Easter trope soon developed into a comical interlude including a race to the tomb by Peter and Andrew; a plethora of additional characters, such as merchants and Romans; and a set of scenes in which Mary Magdalene purchases anointing-oil from an old merchant with a young wife and a lecherous but handsome assistant, Robin. Small wonder that Robin makes a cuckold of the old man – but strange that this should have happened with Church sanction. So popular was the triangle of old man, young wife and lover – which completely overshadowed the liturgy in importance – that Adam de la Halle (1238–88) made a small opera out of it. In an Erlau Easter play, recorded in the fifteenth century, 885 of the 1331 lines concern the love triangle.

As the liturgical play developed it not only became increasingly distant from its supposed roots, but also larger and larger in scale, so that the audience began to find itself literally part of the performance again. Medieval towns were small and most of the huge number of speaking and non-speaking roles called for by the texts had to be assigned to the 'audience'. The Alsfeld play (*c.* 1500) had 172 speaking parts and took three days to perform; a play at Bozen (now Bolzano, Italy) with an extensive cast took seven days to perform; and some plays performed in Frankfurt are recorded as having nearly 1000 speaking and non-speaking roles. This tradition persists in some areas to this day: the famous Oberammergau Passion play takes a whole day, and large numbers of local people participate.

But is Tuitilo's little Easter trope really the source of all this? The size and emphasis of the plays, and their rapid growth, show that the theory of the emergence of modern theatre out of the Easter liturgy is inadequate. Despite all Christian efforts, elements of pre-Christian ritual survived in the popular imagination and the Easter liturgy attempted to harness the 'primitive' energies involved. In this it was unsuccessful, since the secular content of the plays soon outstripped the sacred and when the Church banned them from its doors, the Mystery-play cycles were performed in the streets and the market-place, either on processional carts or on fixed stages set up in a line, to symbolise the various places in which the action occurred – Pilate's Palace, Herod's Palace, the tomb of Christ, the Merchant's shop and so on. As the scene shifted from place to place, so the audience moved with it. It is significant that all this happened at Easter, the traditional time of fertility rites. The rebirth of theatre at this time occurred primarily through audience pressure, and in spite of Church opposition.

Audiences tended strongly to identify performers with their roles, which could make villains' parts dangerous to play. Actors asked to perform figures such as Judas or Pilate would 'play it safe' and merely 'demonstrate' their parts; a similar strategy could also be adopted for playing Christ but for the opposite reason that it might seem blasphemous to be speaking as Christ rather than on his behalf. In this act of distancing lies one route of Bertolt Brecht's model of the alienated actor of epic theatre.

Clearly, the carnival sketches focusing on the natural functions of man, mocking asceticism and providing a raucous and bawdy affirmation of life, spring from the age-old rites associated with the expulsion of winter and welcoming of summer. In this context, the Easter play naturally became a supreme expression of the carnival spirit. Its entirely secular equivalent was the Harlequin play, one of the most persistent and influential of all dramatic genres, with a 'sacrificial victim' as its dominant character.

In Watteau's graceful Harlequin paintings, theatre has completed its passage from primeval beginnings to sublime art. In the primitive rites of public expulsion of winter, 'harlekins' were poor devils driven off by exuberant spring. The diamond pattern of the later Harlequin's costume comes from the dry leaves attached to their clothes. In the course of time, Harlequin ceased to be the poor devil on whom tricks were played and became instead a witty and versatile figure in his own right – the Arlecchino of *Commedia dell'arte*. The origin of his comic misfortunes in the sufferings of a sacrificial victim points to a conceptual affinity between him and Christ in the Easter plays, and emphasises the common origins of tragedy and comedy.

In stressing the close links between the tragic and the comic, Jung refers to a duality in the concept of the divine.[11] Yahweh, for instance, was held to be both benevolent and destructive; the Roman god Janus had two faces; and Hermes/Mercury, messenger of the gods and god of merchants, was tricky and fickle, lending his name to the 'trick-ster' metal mercury. In the medieval Feast of Fools (or Feast of Asses) the farcical penetrated the sphere of the divine. A procession of asses entered the church. Grotesque foolery took place at the high altar. During Mass, the audience imitated the asses, reportedly bray-ing three times in response to the priest's dismissal 'Ite, missa est!' Jung quotes du Cange, who in his *Glossarium mediae et infimae latinatis* relates how mummers with grotesque masks, some dressed up as lions, performed dances and played games in church, sang obscene songs in chorus, wined and dined at a corner of the altar and burned stinking incense made from old shoe-leather.

It took the ecclesiastical authorities half a millenium to suppress such lewdness and debauch. The Church failed to perceive that in the Feast of Fools man presented himself to God in his essential human-ity, with all the shortcomings of human nature. Furthermore, this 'all-too-human' element could not be entirely suppressed and the spirit of the merry-making 'audience' of the Feast of Fools lived on in the characters of the *commedia dell'arte* and other similar entertain-ments. They all enthralled their audiences.

III

It is heartening to see an audience, aroused by a good play, flexing its muscles and going out to fight for something better. One evening in the spring of 1830, the Brussels Opera House was 'full as an egg'; Brussels at the time was occupied by troops of the Netherlands, to which the Belgian provinces had been ceded at the Congress of Vienna. The curtain had risen on Auber's opera *The Silent Woman of Portici*. All awaited the inspiring duet 'Holy love for my fatherland, free should it be, freedom its destiny!' As soon as it had been sung the whole audience stormed out into the streets of Brussels and fought with sticks and stones against the Dutch army of occupation. Belgium became an independent kingdom in the same year.

At one point in Schiller's *Don Carlos*, Marquis Posa squarely confronts Philip of Spain, mainstay of the Inquisition and says, 'Give us the right to think!' At a performance in Hitler's Germany, this one line induced courage, kindled a spirit of resistance and welded the audience together. Goebbels had to stop the play. There was a similar response to the line in 1962, at the time of a scandal involving the then Minister of Defence for West Germany, Franz-Josef Strauss.

Brecht was well aware of the theatre's potential for rousing an audience to action and sought to harness it to bring about a workers' and peasants' utopia. In his concept of 'epic theatre', the spectator must follow a play critically, with controlled emotions, not falling prey to any stage illusions, keen to prevent anything dreadful happening on stage from happening in reality. Above all, the audience must be constantly reminded that the action on stage is make-believe: the tree is just paint and paper; Coriolanus is not Coriolanus but an actor 'demonstrating' this part. Songs, interjected from time to time, sharply break any illusion and drive home the ideological point. Brecht wanted his spectator cool, aloof, unmoved *in* the theatre – yet outside moved to action.

Brecht had great success with audiences, not because of the 'alienation effects' of his epic theatre but rather in spite of them. He was crafty enough not to spoil a play when it was playing to good houses by smashing it against the 'self-imposed dyke' of his alienation effect. Thus, some of his plays, such as *The Threepenny Opera* and *The Good Woman of Setzuan*, have been big box-office successes – *The Threepenny Opera* mainly because of Weill's score, and *The Good Woman of Setzuan* because Brecht fails to find and formulate a clear message and his characters escape control. Yet, message there must be, and at the end of *The Good Woman*, Brecht deals a trick card to the public:

Without good ending, dear audience, this play is going to bust!
Do look for it, there must be one: just must must must!

The audience however, not previously bothered with breaks of illusion and reminders to be prudent, take this one in their stride, as it comes at the end and is nicely rhymed. They clap warmly. Life has been shown as it is. There is no message; this is no new morality play.

Peter Brook relates in his book *The Empty Space* that the stage-designer Gordon Craig, too, rebelled all his life against make-believe theatre, but nevertheless liked painted trees and woods best, and his eyes lit up when he described the effect of a *trompe l'oeil* on an awed audience.

We may safely conclude: the critical actor's 'stepping outside' of his role, the demonstration that sets are no more than paper and paint, Brecht's pricking the balloon of illusion – all these are nothing compared to that magic moment when heart and mind are filled with the emotion and thoughts of an Antigone, a Hamlet, a Don Giovanni, or a Woyzeck. 'Message? Message? What the hell do you think I am, a bloody postman?', replied Brendan Behan curtly when he was asked about the message of his play *The Hostage*.

To make up for the lack of an audience flocking to message theatre, some ensembles take their message to the audience. To their astonished delight, strollers in a park in San Francisco find a band of actors who befriend them and start acting for them. Invariably, when the messages start to trickle from the improvised stage, the spectators trickle away (it is easy in an open park to sneak off). They are not spellbound. 'Message' theatre is messy theatre, and the messages of 'capitalist theatre' (for instance, commercials) fail to fascinate just as much as the messages of 'socialist theatre' do.

IV

Whether facing an elaborate stage or an empty space, an audience is amazingly open, versatile, swift to understand and participate. It will willingly imagine Venice, Birnam Wood, or the appearance of a Japanese ghost. It is able to bear all manner of shock treatment, and it will even readily accept constant changes within a single character, as exemplified by the clown Ringlo in Indian drama.

In India, open-air performances of the *Mahabharata* and *Ramayana* attract large crowds, thought they begin late at night and last until the early hours of the morning. Ringlo is the master of ceremonies, constantly interrupting the action to talk to the audience, filling in missing lines, introducing new characters, and singing the odd couplet from time to time to make it easier for the audience to follow the story. One interesting feature of Ringlo is that he not only keeps a vigilant eye on the audience but also criticises actors if they are late in entrances, or ill-dressed, thus taking the wind out of the audience's sails. Ringlo is not a detached critical figure in the Brechtian mould. Rather he helps re-establish the mood of the play when it has been disturbed; he mends the fragile fabric of illusion when it has been ruptured.[12]

Japanese audiences are ready to accept that a given device may serve different functions, depending on the conventions involved. In both the classical No and less formal Kabuki the stage plan includes a pathway: in No it is called the *Hashigakari* and separates the audience from the actors; in Kabuki it is the *Hanamichi* ('flower path'), which 'favours intimate mutual exchange between stage and audience'[13] – flowers are thrown on the path in honour of favourite actors, and these actors come down the path to chat with their admirers. While it is easy to alienate an audience by treating it as row after row of tailors' dummies sitting in the dark, it is remarkable how much it will permit, and enjoy, in performance when its interest is engaged. Perhaps surprisingly, a play's reception seems to have little to do with whether the audience knows the plot. If anything, seeing a play several times seems to enhance (to use Aristotle's term) the cathartic effect.

In almost any fringe theatre we can see performers looking for new ways to relate to their audience. In some, an attempt is made to establish physical contact: actors may flirt with spectators before they are allowed to take their seats, or a purring actress may adjust a bewildered spectator's tie. In others, the audience members may be invited to jot down a question on a slip of paper: the actors promise that every one of these questions will be brought up during the play, and the audience, in their role as playwright, wait in rapt attention for their respective contributions to be used. In Ensues, near Marseilles, Le Théâtre Western arranges short plays in such a way as to involve the spectators in the action – taking part in train robberies, shoot-outs, Red-Indian dances, and the like.

As long as the audience does not become involved, any theatrical effort is wasted. The spectator who is not moved will just move out. For this reason alone, if for no other, the audience is the most important element in theatre. In Peter Handke's remarkable play *Insulting the Audience* the audience is bluntly informed, 'Sie sind das Thema' ('You are the agenda'). The spectator's expectations, frustrations, attitudes and mannerisms are shown. Throughout, four actors artfully scold the audience for just sitting there without reacting, making no contribution whatever, doing nothing. The audience is put on stage, and constantly attacked for not taking part. When, in a performance I saw, some spectators responded to the insults by shouting back, the actors, good as they were, became puzzled and did not know how to react. So they went on as if they had heard nothing. From the play's point of view it was the best thing they could do. The diction of the play is so artfully construed, the patterns of the rhythmical language so interwoven with the geometry of the actors' movements, that any improvised response would have been likely to have destroyed the delicate fabric of the play.

Two Canadian painters, Bruno and Molly, who went to the performance with me, loved it without understanding a word of the German dialogue: the choreographed movements of the actors (there is no plot), the rhythmical language (Handke evokes the Beatles), the imaginative variations in the grouping of the four young actors communicated a sense of being present at, and participating in, a magical rite. On such occasions, it is the communal experience, the feelings evoked, that count, rather than clear and comprehensible speech. (One thinks again of the way spectators react at a football match.) Yet there is a constraint: genuine and unrestricted audience participation prevents fully effective performance from taking place, even in a play whose subject is the audience.

V

How does the audience perform? This question would once have been answered in a way that science would find exasperatingly inexact, but things have changed. Social scientists have compiled audience profiles, detailing age, sex, social background, educational attainment, financial status and laughing-habits. Applause has been measured, and the responses of individual spectators have been recorded and analysed using a wide variety of research tools, including computerised 'infra-red photographs and telemetry installations recording the course of biological functions in the members of the audience (skin temperature, pulse, perspiration and so on)'.[14]

In the preface to his report on scientific experiments with spectators in theatre Heribert Schälzky[15] insists that aesthetic phenomena can be measured like anything else – that quality can be quantified. To the scientist this is nothing less than the fulfilment of a dream: to make something suspiciously subjective subject to rigorously objective methods of investigation, to render it, finally, explicable. While some hold that Schälzky's experiments have put the whole discipline of theatre research on a sound footing, others argue that all the facts and figures accumulated say little about the scope, the intention, the art and beauty of a play. But now we know that the spectator's breathing is at times synchronised with the actor's. We have statistics on his (or her) social status and income bracket, on his state of mind before, during and after the performance, and even know how often and how loud he laughs. To the question of the audience's laughing-habits a new dimension has been added by the discovery of 'a correlation between the frequency and intensity of audience laughter and the total number of spectators present'.[16]

There is research into categories of laughing: some researchers enumerate seven, while others arrive at 'a total number of eleven non-overlapping processes of laughter'.[17] There is no dispute that there is a registered comic effect when Malvolio, victim of a practical joke, enters in the third act of *Twelfth Night*; but the *type* of comic effect is a matter of great controversy. Whereas 'Gabbard ascribes the comic effect of this moment to (1) Overstatement, (2) Double Meaning (dramatic irony of the fact that the audience and the practical jokers know what is going on but Olivia does not know yet) and (3) Impropriety (the lack of respect for a high household officer)', van den Bergh ascribes it to 'Indirect Confirmation, Contrast, Anticipatory Pleasure and Fulfilment of Expectation'.[18]

While cinema and television audiences have not yet been studied as exhaustively as theatre audiences, it seems clear that we do not usually watch television, for example, in the same way as we watch theatre. How do we watch television? Often with interruptions, so that we consume bits of film much as we nibble snacks while watching. More importantly, films are linear in nature, which is particularly apparent in television series and programmes interrupted by commercials: each bit of action moves to a climax, which stimulates interest in what comes next. In a way, television is comparable to a serialised novel, with some sort of climax at the end of each instalment. The aim is, Scheherazade like, to hold the interest of the audience, without demanding a high level of concentration.

Film has an obvious advantage over theatre here, in that it can achieve far greater realism and call on a much greater range of effects. Cowboys gallop: the *Titanic* sinks; a jumbo jet flies on and on. Theatre cannot do it 'right' to that extent. On the other hand, theatre has its own advantages: the environment favours the subtle build-up of a well-wrought play, as opposed to the linear staccato of television. In the absence of the blunt realism of the screen, a much stronger appeal is made to the audience's imagination; and the audience can itself influence the performance and even participate. For these reasons, seeing a play in a theatre may be far more satisfactory than watching a film on television.

VI

A snack-vendor in a Dutch theatre observed that the more tragic the performance, the less snacks were sold during the interval, and that his sales soared when the audience had seen the actors eat something on stage just before the interval. He therefore urged the actors always to eat something on stage before the interval, and prospered as a result. The audience dug into his snacks.[19]

This imitative consumption of snacks and, we might add, drinks during the interval invites an afterthought. How about the audience's reaction at the end of the show? During the show, the spectator – that isolated individual in the dark – feels, at least in a non-committal way, close to the rest of the audience and shares, at a distance, the feelings of some of the actors. Then the curtain falls and the show is over.

When I worked with a group of actors performing in a hall on an industrial exhibition site, our performance space was not intended for theatre. There was no curtain, and the actors had to leave the hall, along with the spectators. On their way out, some spectators rushed up spontaneously to the performers they had just seen on stage and gave them presents, singling out especially the male lead. They wanted to establish some kind of continuing community between themselves and the actors, above all with the protagonist of the play. They did not want to accept that it was all over, that all community of audience and actors ended with the end of the play. The identification process, once established in performance, cannot easily be stopped. The spectator would like it to continue and looks for the means of achieving this. In like manner, the Amazonian Indian shrinks only the head of a respected warrior whom he wishes to emulate, always keeping his talisman close at hand as it confers the dead man's strength on him.

But what has all this got to do with the role of theatre in our culture? Let's assume that our spectator has sat through the world's longest-running play, Agatha Christie's *The Mousetrap*. The curtain falls. Our man – or woman – will, together with the whole house, applaud warmly. Wondering why such a play goes down so well with audiences, hardly anyone will think of the Omaha Indians or the Eskimo ptarmigans and ducks, or link the play's success to the origins of drama in imitative magic. Yet there it lies. The success of sagas in which the blond, youthful hero defeats evil goblins, of tales in which the gallant knight slays the dragon and rescues the fair maiden in peril, of detective stories in which Hercule(!) Poirot discovers the identity of the murderer and his fiendish schemes is rooted in the audience's craving to see man asserting himself against and defeating destructive forces. It may be difficult to imagine Hercule Poirot tugging at a rope along with sturdy Eskimos or dancing in the round, vigorously spitting, with the Omaha Indians, yet he too is a St George slaying the dragon of winter and freeing from the dragon's clutches the golden-haired princess. With his little grey cells he foils the villain so that Margot or Heather or whatever fair damsel may live on with her very own George in blissful triviality. He is to be cheered.

A much finer piece, Mozart's *Don Giovanni*, is firmly based on the same structural pattern: man asserts himself against the forces of destruction, wresting from its claws the joy of life, defying even death in the end. The lights go on. Don Giovanni meets with an ecstatic ovation. A queue of spectators forms at the stage door waiting for him to appear. He is embraced, has his hand shaken, is congratulated and asked for his autograph. The spectators want to have something in common with him. He is a living link to the reality he has brought to life, filling them with enthusiasm. Don Giovanni represents a larger world they wish to embrace. He indeed is a 'star' whom they want to hitch to their wagon. After *Don Giovanni*, they will go out into the night with a curious feeling of irrational bliss.

NOTES

1. James G. Frazer, *The Golden Bough: A Study in Magic and Religion*, abridged edition (London, 1960) p. 418.
2. Cf. ibid., pp. 416–18 (Battle of Summer and Winter).
3. Ibid., p. 83.
4. Takis Muzenidis, 'The Greek Audience at the Ancient Festivals and Present-Day Festivals', in *Das Theater und sein Publikum*, conference proceedings, Institut für Publikumsforschung der Osterreichischen Akademie der Wissenschaften and Commission Universitaire de la Federation Internationale pour la Recherche Théâtrale, Vienna (1977) p. 134.
5. Frazer, *The Golden Bough*, p. 615.

6. Ibid.
7. Muzenidis, in *Das Theater und sein Publikum*, p. 135.
8. Ibid., p. 136.
9. Ibid.
10. Cf. ibid., p. 146.
11. Cf. C. G. Jung, 'Zur Psychologie der Tricksterfigur', *Die Archetypen und das kollektive Unbewusste* (Olten: Walter, 1976) pp. 273–90.
12. Chandravadan C. Mehta, 'Behaviour of the Open-Air Audience in India', in *Das Theater und sein Publikum*, p. 259.
13. Toshio Kawatake, 'Audience of No and Kabuki, Past and Present', in ibid., p. 262.
14. J. M. Bordewijk-Knotter, 'Empiric Audience Research, its Relevance and Applicability', in ibid., p. 389.
15. Heribert Schälzky, *Empirisch-quantitative Methoden in der Theaterwissenschaft* (Munich: Kitzinger, 1980) pp. 16–17.
16. Analysis summarised from Bordewijk-Knotter, in *Das Theater und sein Publikum*, p. 391.
17. Ibid.
18. Ibid., p. 392.
19. Cf. ibid., p. 388.

Chapter 5

Carnival and the Poetics of Reversal

ANTHONY GASH

'Reversal' is a complex word. It may simply name a logical relation of symmetrical opposition, but shades into more evaluative words which share the Latin root -*vertere* (to turn): *subversion*, which undermines, uproots and destroys; *conversion*, with its Platonic and Christian history of lasting spiritual reorientation; and *perversion*, which, now usually used of sexual behaviour, still retains some of its original connotations of diabolic rebellion against a divinely or-dained natural order – 'women to govern men, sons the fathers, slaves freemen being total violations and perversions of nature and nations'.[1] It is perhaps because they share the complexity of the word that rituals which reverse roles and suspend normal rules of conduct have attracted the attention of anthropologists, historians and semiological theorists. The purpose of this essay is to introduce some of the major issues which have been raised in these disciplines, and to suggest that it is in theatrical performance, which mediates be-tween elite (written, prescribed) and popular (audio-visual, impro-vised) culture, that the paradoxes which originate in popular festivity have found their most conscious and sustained expression.

The conservative function of rituals of status-reversal

As perceived by the anthropologist Max Gluckman, the major paradox of rituals of status-reversal is that, while they appear to enact rebellion, they in fact reproduce and even strengthen the established social order. The 'ritualisation' of existing social roles and relationships through symbolic reversal attempts to show that 'harmony among people can be achieved despite the conflicts, and that social institutions are in fact harmonious – ultimate statements that are belied to some extent by the ritualisation itself'.[2] Two points are elided in this argument. The first is logical: reversals are only intelligible in terms of a normative system of rules, oppositions and subordinations. The ritual enactment of 'opposites' therefore provides a mirror or map of the 'true' order of things. The second point is psychological: to allow interiors to abuse or command superiors is an attempt to exorcise aggressive impulses which might otherwise jeopardise the smooth running of a hierarchical society. The means by which 'ritualisation' controls rebellious impulses are (1) by rigidly prescribing the form that the reversals take, (2) by confining such behaviour to seasonal or life-crisis occasions, where they are believed to have magical efficacy in inducing fertility and prosperity, (3) by joining them to symbolic idealisations of hierarchy (the Zulu king is first insulted and then praised as all powerful; the licence of Carnival is followed by the penance of Ash Wednesday).

A concomitant of this argument is that rituals of reversal characterise cultures with no developed concept of history. The rituals attempt to reduce the real threat of change to the symbolic spectacle of inversion. They imply that, since the only alternative to the *status quo* is complete topsy-turvydom, there can be no middle way of gradual and specific change. Hence they eventually lapse in modern societies where there are political channels for social reform, and where social mobility allows individual independence from collective allegiances.

Gluckman's position has been endorsed by several historians of late medieval and early modern culture – notably Keith Thomas and Charles Phythian-Adams.[3] They demonstrate that indiscriminate puritan castigation of all 'Catholic' and 'pagan' ritual practices has led us to overestimate the degree of anarchy, violence and promiscuity involved in popular festivals, such as the mock-mayorings and misrule of Christmas, the courtship rituals of Mayday, the symbolic rebellions of husbands against wives at Hocktide, and the 'barring-out' of teachers by pupils to mark the start of holidays. We are asked to regard all such expressions of 'misrule' as collusive rituals in which superiors and inferiors freely collaborated; to observe the complementarity within the seasonal calendar of rituals which reversed, and those which idealised, hierarchy; and also to notice the conservative and punitive role of apparently noisy and anarchic practices such as the charivari, which censured shrews and wife-beaters with rough music or by parading offenders backwards on a donkey to symbolise their perversion of natural order.

The subversive potential of festivity

Such arguments, however, are always in danger of seeking to explain what is necessarily a paradoxical form of behaviour by suppressing one co-ordinate of that paradox. Several studies of the role of the crowd in European history (notably those by Natalie Zemon Davis and E. Le Roy Ladurie) have drawn attention to incidents when 'the tension between the festive and everyday official realms was broken and uprising ensued'.[4] In Norwich on Shrove Tuesday (the English equivalent of the European Carnival), 1443, the king of Christmas, attended by 'the twelve months of the year', instead of yielding to Lent 'clad in white and red herring skins in token that sadness should follow any holy time', led a revolt of citizens against the local landowning abbot who was threatening to close two of their mills.[5] During the revolt of the Netherlands in Cambrai, the rebels were costumed and carried fools' sceptres topped with effigies of a hated governor.[6] And an entire popular uprising, against government and taxes, and its brutal suppression by the local nobility took place at the Mardi Gras celebrations at Romans in 1580, 'with theatrical and ritual gestures leading up to the final massacre'.[7]

Even as late as 1842 in Wales, the traditional transvestite masquerade of mummers' plays and May games provided both symbolism and camouflage for the 'Rebecca' riots against the authority that centralised British government exerted in the shape of new turnpike tolls and poor laws.[8] All these incidents show that the traditional seasonal licence to criticise unjust rule, to exorcise accumulated social evil, and to inhabit a utopian upside-down world set free from hierarchy and material scarcity could, at times of social crisis, be used as a legitimation of political rebellion against unjust authority or innovation.

Bakhtin's theory of carnival

Given that the traditional fertility symbolism of turning the world upside-down has been periodically used to camouflage and legitimate rebellion, it can be inferred that, even when no violence ensued, the game of social levelling and anti-authoritarian parody always had the potential for self-parody, raising at every moment the question of its precise degree of jest or earnest. To reverse or travesty power relations in a spirit of holiday laughter is implicitly to foster an awareness that even the normal, workaday hierarchy is itself a kind of fiction, susceptible of change or of assuming other forms of expression.

The account of popular festivity which is most responsive to this potential for jesting equivocation is by Mikhail Bakhtin, who was himself schooled in irony by the intimidating and monolithic dogmas of Stalinism. In two outstanding works which relate fundamental questions about the political nature of language to the practice of individual writers, *Problems of Dostoyevsky's Poetics* and *Rabelais and his World*, Bakhtin extends the term 'carnival' to designate all forms of symbolic reversal undertaken in the spirit of laughter. He notes that the logic of topsy-turvydom (a continuous shifting from top to bottom, from front to rear'[9]) informed market-place celebrations of many of the major medieval Church festivals, such as the Feast of Circumcision (the Feast of Fools), Shrovetide (Carnival) and Easter (Easter Laughter). The sane logic is also active in popular oaths, in rhymes about the utopian land of Cockayne, in chapbook prints and inn signs and in an extensive repertoire of parodies of sermons, gospels, wills and ecclesiastical decrees. Bakhtin is thus able to posit the existence of a resourceful medieval parodic world or oral counterculture, which the peasantry (often joined by the lower clergy and by students) welcomed any opportunity to inhabit and embellish. It thrived in its resistance to the more repressive and terrifying doctrines of organised Christianity, and, during the Reformation, fertilised humanist serio-comedy (Erasmus, More, von Hutten, Rabelais) in its satire of scholastic conservatism and its utopian celebrations of man's capacity to transform himself and his environment.

Identifying rituals of crowning and discrowning, burial and revival, as the primary carnival performances, Bakhtin suggests that 'carnival', far from simply mirroring a static and hierarchical order, 'celebrates change itself, the very process of replaceability, rather than that which is replaced. Carnival is so to speak not substantive. It absolutizes nothing; it proclaims the jolly relativity of all things.'[10] Thus he refuses socially or magically functional explanations of reversal, and considers it as a kind of serious game which exposes the distinction between form and content which ruling ideologies seek to conceal. To profane, through laughter, the forbidding symbols of divine and political power is to expose them as *merely* symbols, and thus to throw into doubt the tragic and sacrificial world-view which they enshrine.

Key terms in Bakhtin's theory are *mésalliance, ambivalence* and *the grotesque concept of the body.*

Mésalliance is the process whereby 'all things that were closed off, isolated, and separated from each other enter into carnivalistic contacts and combinations'.[11] At festivals, people are liberated from criteria of estate, rank, age and property status to enter into free and familiar contact in a shared space. Likewise parodies and profanities, oral, theatrical and written, combine and juxtapose the sacred with the profane, high and low styles, Latin and the vernacular, erudition and obscenity.

Ambivalence refers to the Janus-faced symbolism of rituals which was initially associated with seasonal or personal transitions – the solstices, funerals, and so on. The term covers hybrid images (pregnant death, the gay funeral, the church as a tavern, or hell's mouth as a festive kitchen) and paired opposites chosen for contrast (fat Carnival versus emaciated Lent; giants and dwarves) or for similarity (doubles and twins). Parody is the verbal equivalent of such two-in-one images because, in parody, 'the word becomes the arena of conflict between two voices',[12] as the words of one speaker are forced to serve purposes diametrically opposed to his own. Carnivalesque iconography implies a world derived not from a single divine authority but from a continuous interaction of opposing forces. Likewise, carnivalesque language subverts rhetorical claims to authority or objectivity by treating *all* language as dialogue. (Even authoritarian monologue bears the imprint of the sceptical voice which it strives to exclude.) 'Ambivalence' also refers to the fact that the negations of folk humour are always tied to a principle of regeneration. To degrade official discourse by associating it with the imagery of eating, drinking, copulation, defecation and pregnancy is symbolically to transform what was abstract into 'flesh and matter'[13] and thus to renew it.

The idea of ambivalence leads directly to the postulation of an aesthetic canon of the *grotesque* uniting all carnival practices in an *image of the body* so constituted as to be inimical to the classical cultivation of harmony and proportion.[14] Grotesque symbolism dismembers the body, exaggerates its protuberances and apertures and draws attention to bodily processes. Often the processes are treated as integral in images of pregnant death, or excremental banquets. The effect of such imagery is both to 'bury and revive' because it assaults the sense of a bounded and private selfhood, while simultaneously celebrating the capacity of 'the collective ancestral body of all the people'[15] eternally to renew itself.

Theatre and festivity

Bakhtin has not gone unchallenged. In a balanced appraisal of his critical influence, Peter Stallybrass and Allon White point out that adherence to Bakhtin's model can lead to an unreflective and nostalgic populism which shuts its eyes to carnival's abuse and demonisation of weaker, social groups,[16] while M. A. Screech, placing Rabelais in a humanist, courtly culture, points out that many of his excremental allusions have critical rather than celebratory connotations.[17] Whatever the defects of Bakhtin's social or literary history, however, I shall argue that his method works well for the theatre, an area which he himself neglected.[18] In England during the fifteenth and sixteenth centuries, for example, the commercialisation and secularisation of performance allowed first the travelling professionals and then the new London theatres to develop the festive idiom while freeing it from those humiliations of the weak and idealisations of the powerful which rituals themselves entailed. In observing this process, we need to keep in mind the differences between rituals and plays as well as their similarities.

First, plays explore the relationship between individuals and roles, while rituals deal only in formalised roles. An audience's response to Shylock, for example, however hostile, is tempered by reflections on how the world looks to him: he is given a voice, which cannot be said of those Jews who were annually forced into a race and stoned at the Roman Carnival.[19] Secondly, while the ceremonial year in the Middle Ages alternated between those rituals which idealised hierarchy and those which inverted norms, the theatre draws its boundaries more teasingly. When, for example, 'King Hal' heads the coronation procession at the end of *Henry IV, Part 2* or when the Duke stages a triumphal entry and public trial at the end of *Measure for Measure*, the festive opponents of authority (Falstaff, Lucio) reappear to interrupt the solemnities in a way which would have been unthinkable in the actual rituals of state which the plays 'quote'. Thirdly, while in rituals the representatives of rule and misrule are always distinguishable, the theatre has another trick to play. Unsupported by military force, and unadorned by conspicuous wealth, the 'King', 'magistrate', or 'priest', 'dressed in a little brief authority' (*Measure for Measure*, II.ii.118) is also a player, as powerless as the clown. Thus the doubleness which is only embryonic in ritual becomes the basis of theatre, where every coronation, marriage or trial is, by definition, a mock-coronation, mock-marriage or mock-trial. 'Mock-' does not always mean mocking. Theatrical ambivalence can be made to work in contrasting directions: either an intimidating social ritual can be demystified, or, conversely, a secular fiction may be infused with a ritualistic solemnity. When theatre is at its most complex, as in Richard II's reversal of the coronation ceremony (*Richard II*, IV.i), the only scene in Shakespeare which we know to have been censored, the two possibilities coexist.

Unfortunately, distinctions between theatre and ritual have been insufficiently observed in critical studies of 'festive comedy'. The two classic studies of this kind, C. L. Barber's *Shakespeare's Festive Comedy* (1959) and Ian Donaldson's *The World Upside-Down* (1970) are subtle in their readings of individual plays, but tend to equate ritual and drama in the proposition that 'misrule works through the whole dramatic rhythm of the play, to consolidate rule'.[20] This doctrine has recently re-emerged among the new historicists. Leonard Tennenhouse in a chapter called 'Staging Carnival' asserts that 'we have to consider the Elizabethan drama as a forum for staging symbolic shows of state power, and as a vehicle for disseminating court ideology'.[21] Such declarations, in denying autonomy to theatrical expression, mark, in my view, a regression from the stance of two English contemporaries of Bakhtin, William Empson and A. P. Rossiter, who, though they had no access to Bakhtin's writings, often parallel his approach.[22] Both were keenly interested in parodic subplots, and regarded the best of medieval and Renaissance drama as characteristically ambivalent or dialectical in its structure. This sort of ambiguity was related by Empson to divisions of opinion within the audience: 'The supreme case of dramatic ambiguity is Verrall's interpretation of Euripides: the plays were to dramatize sacred myths for a popular religious festival, yet for some members of the audience they were to suggest criticism of the gods, for others to convey complete disbelief and actually rationalize the myths before their eyes.'[23]

In response to an audience of mixed social composition, the topic of the world upside-down often becomes ambiguous in a similar way. The spectrum of associations which a carnivalesque play can elicit from an audience, either simultaneously or in sequence, can be conveniently divided into comic *reversal*, political *subversion*, diabolic *perversion* and mystical *conversion*. The dramatic critic needs to ask, is a given incident merely a comic *reversal* which coming in the middle of a play triggers the conventional expectation of a return to order, or is it a signal for a more fundamental questioning of received values? The former is essentially Barber and Donaldson's view: they work in terms of a strict generic restriction to comedy – not, for example, taking on the image of the world upside-down in generic hybrids such as *Measure for Measure* or *King Lear*. Their case is premised on the neo-Aristotelian assumption that a play can be regarded as an organic process which moved, as Barber puts it, 'through release to clarification': that is, one progresses through the mood of holiday anarchy back towards a more workaday sense of the world, having banished extremes, and learnt to take the claims of nature into account.[24]

It is likely, however, that theatrical images of reversal have often encouraged more *subversive* reflections on ruling conceptions of order than this account allows. It is worth noting that Marx and Engels frequently employ similes of reversal in formulating their critique of 'ideology'. Legal, philosophical and moral abstractions, they argue, tend to erase their own origins in lived social processes and conflicts by mistakenly assuming the priority of consciousness over material existence. The result is that 'in all ideology men and their relations appear upside-down as in a *camera obscura*'.[25] The critique of ideology seeks to invert the inverted world of ideology by recontextualising ideas within the exploitative system of material production which conditions them and which they, often unconsciously, seek to justify and perpetuate. Brecht makes the symmetry between Marxist dialectics and comedy central to his conception of theatrical 'alienation' – the 'making strange' of ideologically conditioned behaviour. Azdak's topsy-turvy court in *The Caucasian Chalk Circle*, which unmasks legal principles as ideological reflections of economic relations, is modelled on Sancho Panza's governorship in *Don Quixote*. It shows with how little strain festive reversal can become the incognito of ideological critique.

A third possibility is for the image of reversal to symbolise a *perversion* of a divinely ordained norm which threatens to sever the harmonious bonds of human society to nature and to divinity. Clytemnestra's 'masculinity' and her inversion of ritual forms when she 'sacrifices' Agamemnon come under this heading,[26] as do images of witches and devils as God's parodists which we can trace through medieval drama to Jonsonian masque and the 'Fair is foul, and foul is fair' of *Macbeth*.[27]

Finally, if human consciousness is regarded as fallen or limited, then the reversal of the human world can become a symbolic means of recovering an unfallen, unlimited vision. In the theatre, as in certain rituals, the experience of continuous reversal can be designed to erode the audience's confidence in the categories which filter their 'normal' experience, thus creating a state of mind which welcomes paradox as its most adequate expression. We find a relevant conception of *conversion* in Plato, where man, trapped in the cave of the senses and morally blinded by considerations of social prestige, can only be released from spiritual bondage by an intellectual 'conversion' which orients him towards the Ideal Forms and is compared to 'turning the whole body'.[28] Likewise, Erasmus's ironical *Praise of Folly* (a significant influence of Shakespearian and Jonsonian comedy) appeals to both the New Testament and to Plato in picturing spiritual reality as the invisible opposite of natural, social, and rational appearances: 'all human affairs are like the figure of Silenus described by Alcibiades (Plato: *Symposium*, 215b) and have two completely opposite faces, so that what is death at first sight, as they say, is life if you look within and vice versa . . . the same applies to riches and poverty, obscurity and fortune, learning and ignorance . . . in fact you'll find everything reversed if you open the Silenus'.[29] Here the ideology is specifically Christian, but ritual attempts to cross the boundary of the profane world into a reversed, sacred order, where 'death is converted into birth', may be primitive and universal.[30]

A single play need not be committed to any one of these interpretative schemata, and it is precisely by playing off one schema against another that the theatre has been instrumental in freeing the imagery of reversal from the semantic restrictions which ritual contexts impose or attempt to impose. My main examples of plays which counterpoint or superimpose different meanings of reversal – the ludicrous and the regenerative, the diabolic and the sceptical, the materialist and the mystical, and so on – will be Aristophanes' *Lysistrata* (411 BC), the medieval morality play *Mankind* (1465–70), Shakespeare's *Twelfth Night* (1599–1600) and *Measure for Measure* (1604), and Georg Büchner's *Woyzeck* (1835–6). The purpose of surveying so wide a field is not to chart direct influences, but rather to suggest the universality and adaptability of the logic of reversal: social and conceptual systems fluctuate, but man's need to relativise whatever categories have moulded his experience by 'straining his symbolic faculties to the utmost' (Nietzsche)[31] persists.

Aristophanes and regenerative reversal

The Greek 'old comedy', performed at the Dionysiac festivals of fifth-century Athens, depended on a logic of *mésalliance* very like the carnivalesque idiom of a later period. The comedian with his exaggerated phallus and gaping mask was a licensed transgressor of cultural boundaries. He could fly to Olympus (*Peace*) and even be enthroned as a new Zeus (*Birds*). Dressed as Dionysus he could descend to Hades (*Frogs*). Disguised as a woman he could enter a religious festival restricted to women (*Thesmophoriasuzai*), and conversely he could bring women into the democratic assembly from which they were axiomatically excluded (*Ecclesiasuzai*). He could even cross political frontiers which had been closed by war to negotiate himself a private peace (*Acharnians*). One current critical reading of these plays is as 'holiday escapes from reality'.[32] An older, discredited view saw them as derived from sacrificial ritual.[33] By invoking Bakhtinian terms we can point to a kind of seriousness which is ritualistic but anti-sacrificial in character. (Several of the plays indeed contain parodies of animal sacrifice, which was the cornerstone of all official ceremonial.) The plays symbolically renew the Athenian city state, by immersing the entire society and its formal institutions in the regenerative abyss of the grotesque.

The regenerative symbolism of *reversal* is never clearer than in *Lysistrata*, which was composed by the Lenaian Festival of 411 BC at a time when Athens' survival was seriously threatened by the war with Sparta following the loss of her fleet and the defection of her allies. We might describe the design of the play as a whole as a brilliant pun between bawdy farce (the women go on a sex-strike; the men agree to make peace to assuage their permanent erections), and as sublime mythic pattern – the birth of Harmonia (here represented by a naked slave girl) from the union of Ares (War) and Aphrodite (Love).

The play pivots around a scene of symbolic chaos when the world is turned entirely upside down (pp. 93–100).[34] The women of Athens have taken over the Acropolis, the apex of the city and the nucleus of her empire, in protest at the war between Athens and Sparta. They proceed to silence a Proboulos, one of the newly appointed advisory committee to the Assembly, first by making him hold a spindle and a wool basket and wear a veil, and finally by laying him out as a corpse in a parody of funeral rites. Speakers and listeners, apex and base, government and governed, male and female, sacred and profane, life and death have swapped places. The scene illustrates precisely Bakhtin's (and the anthropologist Victor Turner's[35]) view of the regenerative and healing symbolism of reversal, for the Proboulos represents on one level the warmongering of the democratic Assembly (the preserve of men from which women were excluded) and, on another, the hope that the relatively new advisory committee (established after the disastrous Sicilian defeat) will be able to control the militarism of the Assembly and work towards lasting peace with Sparta. The shortsightedness of the past must be transformed into the wisdom of the future.

The Proboulos stamps into the arena determined to solve the problems posed by the women's revolt in the typical Athenian way – by violence. He ridicules the women by giving another example of women's typically 'uncontrollable behaviour' (p. 93): only the other day, he relates, there was a drunken woman up on the roof lamenting for Adonis, exactly when her husband was boring everyone in the Assembly by making a speech demanding the launching of a new expeditionary force. The irony is that he draws entirely the wrong inference from what he describes. What he portrays as routine male boringness is collective suicide. What he portrays as female drunkenness is divine inspiration which expresses the tragedy of the daily slaughter of Athenian youth: 'weep for Adonis!' (p. 93).

One section of the audience is allowed to laugh at the ridiculous pretensions of women, while another perceives that it is the real political world of Athens which is upside-down and in danger of collapse. On the deepest level, the contrary behaviour of husband and wife is symbolic of a general dissociation of religious values (symbolised as female) and political conduct (male). What then happens to this representative of power, violence and division? It is not enough to say that he is ridiculed. Symbolically he is made to listen to the advice of inferiors rather than be intoxicated by his own rhetoric. He is made to acknowledge his common nature with the whole community by being dressed as a woman, and finally he is laid out as a corpse before stamping off in a kind of grotesque rebirth.

Conversely Lysistrata takes on the role of community and tradition, by lamenting as a mother the human cost of war, by demanding

unity amongst Athenians, and finally by appealing to the on-stage
and actual audience to remember the common religious traditions
which have been severed by war:

> You! who have hallowed altars from one and the same ewer,
> Like blood relations at Olympia –
> Thermopylae – Delphi . . .   (p. 118)

Here, as is often the case in rituals which invest women with the
trappings of authority, 'women' represent universal kinship, which
transcends all boundaries and conflicts.[36] Even the bawdy episodes
where the women comically show their 'true nature' by being unable
to maintain their chastity are ambivalent in the Bakhtinian sense. One
of the women, for example, simulates pregnancy to get back to the
embraces of her husband. When challenged by the iron-willed
Lysistrata, she reveals from under her shift the 'baby' – Athene's
helmet supposedly stolen from the colossal statue which towered
over the Acropolis: this is surely an example of Bakhtin's regenerative grotesque – a forbidding symbol of empire and war is debased
and regenerated by association with the common lower stratum of
physical life (pp. 104–5).

   The play ends with what is apparently a return to proper order and
hierarchy, celebrated in a triptych of beautiful choral hymns: the
gods, who have often been profaned in the course of the play, are
duly honoured, and the men are invited to *lead* their wives in the
dances. But even this image of order cunningly deceives the eye, for
in the apparent return to real life an element of the utopian fantasy is
sustained to the last: the dancers represent both Athenians and Spartans,
who in the real world were mercilessly at war, honouring their
common gods. The audience must have been divided in their response: some would have been moved by the beautiful invocation of
traditional values; others might have resented the propaganda for a
Panhellenic policy dressed up as religion, suspecting, as the old men
have said in one of the earlier parodic battles, that the peace initiative
is 'a plot to establish a tyranny' (p. 101) – a not unreasonable view,
since when the play was performed precisely such a plot – anti-
democratic and pro-Spartan – was afoot.[37]

Mankind and festive perversion

As O. B. Hardison has pointed out, the various types of medieval play

(Corpus Christi cycles, morality plays, liturgical plays) are organised around a persistent 'ritual form' – pathos, peripeteia (reversal), theophany, – which enacts the conversion of the soul or the world from alienation and despair to joy and rebirth through Christ's mercy.[38] Theatrical Vices and devils are the perverters of man's spiritual impulses who try to lure man away from conversion, but are always finally ridiculed and damned for their pains. This evaluation was complicated in performance by the festive and political implications of parody and reversal. *Mankind* (1465–70) provides the fullest surviving example of this kind of complication.[39] The fact that the play was probably performed on Shrove Tuesday, or on other occasions during the winter holiday period, allowed the idea of a festive battle between clean Lent and bawdy Carnival to be counterpointed against the orthodox morality-play struggle between good and evil. The play contains, for example, an excremental Christmas song with the refrain 'Holyke, holyke, holyke!' (holy and lick-hole – 1.344), an inverted blessing ('I blysse you with my left hand: foul you befall!' – l. 522), an obscene parody of a papal pardon (ll. 143–6), a mock beheading and resurrection (ll. 445–7), and an extended parody of a manorial court in which the ten commandments are reversed, and lechery is exempted from the seven deadly sins (ll. 667–725).[40]

Now one possibility is to regard the reversing-idiom of the Vices as evidence that they are inspired by the Devil, and the official view as expressed by Mercy is precisely that. He warns Mankind that the Vices will 'perverte' his condition (l. 296). On this reading, the mock-trial becomes a terrifying prefiguration of the Last Judgements, and eternal damnation. But this fails to recognise that performance tends to undermine allegory. Though all the actors represent agencies of good and evil within the soul, they must have modelled their performances on social roles and relationships which would have been recognisable to the rural East Anglian audience. Mercy, who in more orthodox plays is portrayed as one of the daughters of God, is here a churchman who preaches an intimidating jargon of 'Englysch Latyn' (l. 124). The Vices are tavern carousers and petty criminals. Mankind is a labourer who tills the Church's lands for little or no material reward and can seldom find time for church-going. Hence one aim of the Vices' jokes is to throw into doubt Mercy's divine authority, and to stress instead his temporal power. When Mercy announces his allegorical identity, New Gyse responds with a stark challenge: 'Ye are a strong, cunnyng, clerke' (l. 128). Furthermore the Vices constantly ridicule the Latinate style of official discourse, suggesting that it is used to mystify and intimidate the illiterate majority (e.g. ll. 29–46, ll. 680–1). Indeed, the spectacle of Mankind the ploughman with a spade in one hand and a quill in the other (l. 315), as he writes down a Latin text, tends, in its incongruity, to support their attitude. Finally when Mercy goes off in search of errant Mankind, the Vices treat him like a priest seeking a writ of arrest from a sheriff (ll. 780–1).

In this sense the Vices are social satirists hinting at political motives for priestly conduct. They are also festive revellers in that they transgress boundaries and undermine hierarchies. Mercy's preaching insists that the soul must govern the body and draws an absolute distinction between the damned and the saved. By contrast the Vices elevate the body through obscenities, puns and somersaults, and transgress social boundaries by trying to lure the priest down from his preaching-position to join their dance; by getting the audience to join them in singing the scatalogical Christmas song in canon; and by taking a collection from the audience prior to the appearance of the devil Titivillus, who was obviously a star turn (ll. 459–61). Analogously their nonsensical patter levels conceptual boundaries; they counter the dubiously named Mercy's separation of corn from chaff (saved from damned) (l. 43) by praising corn, chaff and straw as all equally necessary to the agricultural cycle: 'Corn servit bredibus, chaffe horsibus, straw fyrybusque' (ll. 53–7). It is typical of medieval clowning to subvert official ideology at the point where it is most cruel – namely, where it threatens damnation. Another kind of symbolic levelling may have been attained by the doubling of the opposite roles of Mercy and the devil Titivillus by the same actor. In this way God and the Devil share a common body in the most literal sense.

The result of the Vices' festive humour, however, is by no means a simple victory for the humanity of Carnival over the austerity of Lent. The Vices' dual role as clowns and criminals makes them as difficult to evaluate as the crafty churchman who is also Christian Mercy. It is precisely the sort of play in which audience sympathies can vacillate from performance to performance and even from moment to moment. And it is in this ambivalence that its theatricality resides. Its most complex moments occur towards the end of the play. The mock-trial, which is festive because it refers to February (Carnival time), refuses all authority ('in the year of the reign of no king' – l. 693) and all rules (by parodying the commandments), moves the audience to wild laughter. Immediately afterwards, Mercy enters as

Mankind exits to play football. He is distraught with grief. For the first time we see a spiritual, maternal aspect to a figure who has previously seemed secular, patriarchal and harsh (ll. 734–71). In this sharp juxtaposition of the contradictory claims of unbounded nature (the mock-court) and ascetic spirituality (Mercy's grief), both expressed with equal energy, the play attains its most complete freedom from its own didactic conventions. It is as if Christianity, purified by the friction with Carnival, had emerged momentarily from the prison of the Church.

Shakespeare versus Aristotle

In stressing the complex dialectics of plays which are firmly rooted in festive practices and popular idiom, I have been implicitly at odds with Aristotelian assumptions about drama, assumptions which recur whenever plays are discussed primarily in terms of character and plot with little regard to their performance on the stage. I now want to make that disagreement explicit, and, in so doing, to demonstrate that Shakespeare, inheritor of the carnivalesque culture of the Middle Ages, brought some of its institutions into philosophical and political consciousness by exploring the nature of the theatrical medium in a direction quite counter to that proposed by Aristotle.

Carnival versus verisimilitude

Aristotle regards drama as, at best, a transparent mirror of nature, which must accordingly be governed by the proprieties of social life: 'it is not appropriate that a female character be given manliness or cleverness'.[41] He sees its power as residing in a natural 'probability' or poetic truth which is at odds with theatricality: 'The power of tragedy is independent both of performance and actors'.[42] Shakespeare, on the other hand, celebrates the inherent doubleness of the physically present actors and the social roles that they promiscuously assume, in such a way as to make the stage into a subversive metaphor for the equivocations and ultimate emptiness of role-playing in social and political life.

When on the basis of the equivocal relationship between the physically present actors and their assumed roles, a set of quasi-social roles is first established and then reversed – the 'girl' is disguised as a boy

(*Twelfth Night*, or Jonson's *The Silent Woman*), Justice dons the habit of a fool (Jonson's *Bartholomew Fair*), the fool plays the king (Falstaff in *Henry IV Part 1*) or sleeps with the fairy queen (*A Midsummer Night's Dream*), or the king becomes a fool (*King Lear*) – the intrinsic doubleness of actor and role becomes an object of scrutiny and fascination, which raises the question of whether there is a continuous self which survives the metamorphoses of experience. We are tempted to look backwards or forwards to the 'true' identity of the disguised actor, but in doing so we face only an infinite regress. Even in the conclusions of comedies, the conventional unmasking is a discontinuous opposite to the disguised existence which we have experienced throughout the play rather than its organic fulfilment. Barber, then, it seems to me, could not be more wrong than when, claiming that 'when norms are secure then playful aberration is benign', he sees Viola's indelible femininity showing through her disguise.[43] In taking this view he is in danger of making 'Viola' – whose very name is a near-anagram of the name of the other heroine, 'Olivia' – into the heroine of a George Eliot novel who has a biography and grows morally through her tribulations. If he is aware of *Twelfth Night* in performance, what has provided him with his 'security' may be the presence of the actress's body and voice, a security which was unavailable to the Elizabethan audience. On the contrary, it is surely the case that the disjunction between the young man who plays the part and the girl whom he portrays is rendered problematic by the further disguise:

> As I am man,
> My state is desperate for my master's love;
> As I am woman – now alas the day! –
> What thriftless sighs shall poor Olivia breathe!
> (II. ii. 33–7)[44]

Such verbal antitheses draw into consciousness the paradoxical fusion of actor and role which takes place in every performance, and here takes the virtuoso form of the actor's revelation of his own femininity. These verbal antitheses, by bringing us back to the doubleness of the actual and the imagined, encourage us to glimpse the metamorphic power of our own minds. To put all this in terms of the divided audience, we might venture that homosexuals will perceive the play quote differently from heterosexuals. One group is watching a play about homosexual desire and transvestism;[45]

the other a romantic comedy resolved by marriage. These disparate responses are punningly harmonised in the audience as a whole, whose minds meet in laughter and wonder at the extraordinary spectacle of *androgynous* beauty – which, as successive scenes demonstrate, is responded to with equal zest by men (Antonio) and by women (Olivia).

The marriages at the end are typically perfunctory and jocular, but the reunion of the impossible twins (who are supposedly both identical and of different sexes) is accounted dignity by a poetry of wonder and mystical illumination similar to that of the recognition scenes in the last plays, when the vertiginous tempo of the crescendo of comic misunderstandings slows almost to a standstill:

> Do I stand there? I never had a brother
> Nor can there be that deity in my nature
> Of here and everywhere.
>
> (v.i.218–20)

The logical paradox symbolised in Viola (two in one, man and woman) is thus, as it were, projected into space as a visual paradox:

> One face, one voice, one habit, and two persons!
> A natural perspective, that is and is not.
>
> (v.i.208–9)

The paradox, not its resolution, is what induces wonder. Thus the audience – knowing that there are in reality two actors, and knowing that on the level of plot there is a 'logical' explanation of events (brother and sister are identical twins) – are invited to interpret what is present to their eyes as a symbol of a higher order of experience than either the senses or the Aristotelian logic of non-contradiction can attain. In this sense they are invited to climb the Platonic ladder of similitude – using their imaginations to ascend from the dross of sensory particulars towards the form of ideal Beauty which, to use the Platonic style of allegory, the soul remembers having seen when, before birth, it saw the Ideal Forms unveiled.[46] Androgyny is one of the Platonic symbols of the transcendence of man's fallen and divided condition.[47]

I am making two points. One is that it is not social norm or hierarchy that is accorded the status of truth: 'the monstrous' (Viola describes herself as a 'monster' – ii.ii.32 – because she is neither man nor woman) proves to be central, even sacred, while norms of sexual behaviour are comically exposed as abstractions in a utopian or carnival world (Illyria, the stage) which celebrates eccentricity by parading a variegated sexual spectrum from the narcissistic Duke to the 'Amazonian' Maria. The second is that it is the interplay of different levels of sign and meaning – actual (the comings and goings of actors on the stage), fictional (the characters and their social world), and allegorical (nothing is what it seems) – which generates complex and unforeseen meanings. When (in IV.ii) Malvolio is incarcerated under the stage and Feste assails him with his nonsense patter, while alternating roles between priest and clown, *actually* Malvolio's body is invisible to the audience and we hear only his voice, while on the stage another actor doffs and dons costumes and mimics verbal styles. On the level of Aristotelian probability we *place* what is going on – Malvolio the steward is being deceived by Feste the household fool; and on quite another level, which bypasses the preceding altogether, we are disturbed by what we actually see and hear and struggle to interpret it – we glimpse a dream-like world, unbound by causality, where Malvolio *is* a disembodied spirit, in purgatory but still clinging to the ego which he calls his 'soul' (IV.ii.54), while Feste is a devil–priest who through his own protean role-playing (which is most disturbing of all when he plays at being 'Feste'), his nonsense patter and his sly allusion to Pythagorean metempsychosis (IV.ii.49) exposes all worldly attachments to the self, the senses and social status as mental delusions.

CLOWN. Say'st thou that house is dark?
MALVOLIO. As hell, Sir Topas.
CLOWN. Why it hath bay windows transparent as barricadoes and the clerestories towards the south-north are lustrous as ebony, and yet complainest thou of obstruction! (IV.ii.34–8)

In the relativistic world of 'What You Will', however, even the protean clown can be outstripped by experience, as when, confronting the other twin, Sebastian, who denies that he is Cesario (fictional), he thrusts his finger to his nose (presence) and says, '– nor this is not my nose neither!' (IV.i.8–9). Even noses can be dissolved by the imagination.

Such is Shakespeare's freedom from system that he can exploit the discontinuity between social role, theatrical role and physical presence in both Platonic and anti-Platonic directions. In political plays, he is likely to do the latter. In the two parts of *Henry IV*, Falstaff's round belly which dominates the stage becomes an abiding-point of gestic reference, by means of which he identified himself with 'the collective ancestral body of the people' (Bakhtin) and challenges the political abstractions of law, honour and kingship, which should according to the Platonic scheme be closer to the Ideal Forms than the delusive sphere of the sensible. The play is full of parodic references to 'shadows', which means actors or images, and connotes the Platonic cave where worldly values are only spectral similes of a transcendent order. 'Shadow' is usually paired with 'substance', image with reality. While the official view takes the king to be an image of god on earth, and his subjects to be lesser images of him, Falstaff inverts the hierarchy by treating his own belly as true 'substance' and the king's administrators, such as the Lord Chief Justice (Justice on earth), as mere shadows – role-players who repress humanity, theirs and others – in the service of an illusion.

The tavern scene where 'the tun of man' (II.iv.434) who is 'the whole world' (II.iv.463) plays the part of the king with a stool for a throne, a cushion for a crown, and a lead dagger for a sceptre, perfectly illustrates Bakhtin's point about carnival 'crowning and discrowning' where the symbols of authority become 'bilevelled', while 'in the non-carnival world they are absolute, weighty, and monolithically serious'. 'From the outset the discrowning shows through the crowning.'[48] And what makes the traditionally carnivalesque routine so politically subversive in this context is that the true 'king' – Bolingbroke/Henry IV – is himself a 'counterfeit' (v.iii.28) both as a usurper and as a political actor: a Machiavel. Thus, in the climactic battle scene of *Henry IV Part 1* the rebel Douglas, who has ranted that he will 'murder all his wardrobe piece by piece, / Until I meet the king' (v.v.26), is like an enraged metaphysician run mad, pealing the layers of the world onion, to find nothing at its centre. It is in this context that Falstaff, whom the audience believes dead, heaves his fat belly up from the stage, invoking the traditional festive resurrection of folk plays. He is thus making a parodic counter-claim to metaphysical Platonism, or at least its appropriation by kings. It is the body which constitutes the only abiding reality, and survival which constitutes the only necessary value: 'to counterfeit dying, when a man thereby liveth, is to be no counterfeit, but the true and perfect image of life itself' (v.iv.119–22). Here, the paradox is that, *pace* Plato, the true image of life cancels all images: it is the body itself.

In the political world of the histories – unlike in the utopian world
of comedy – there can be no reconciliation of the claims of courtly
and festive culture; there is no equivalent of androgyny to unite the
divided audience. Hence the two parts of *Henry IV* are dialectical in
structure, and reach no higher synthesis. The penultimate scene of
Henry IV Part 2, the one before Hal's coronation and his rejection of
Falstaff, shows a squabble between Doll Tearsheet (a whore) and a
beadle which is both very grim and very funny: Doll is accused as an
accessary to murder, and inverts the roles by threatening the beadle
with justice and hanging. She abuses her captor as a Lenten figures:
'you filthy famished correctioner . . . you starved bloodhound . . .
Goodman death, goodman bones!' (v.iv.21, 27, 28). The Carnival–
Lent contrast is reinforced visually by, on the one hand, Doll's belly
with a cushion on it and, on the other, the skinny beadle.[49] The row
could go on for ever. The antagonism between the common body and
authority is only intensified by the official restitution of order.

Carnival versus 'plot'

Another 'Aristotelian' principle which carnivalesque aesthetics contest is, as I have frequently hinted, the principle of *plot* regarded as a
causally linked series of events which is only fully unfolded at the
end of a play, when it becomes clear that individual actions have been
contributing unawares to a unified and predetermined design. For
Aristotle, *reversal* is a single phase in an organic, continuous and
irreversible sequence. 'A complex action is one in which the change
[of fortune] is accompanied by a discovery or reversal or both. These
should develop out of the structure of the plot, so that they are the
inevitable or probable consequence of what has gone before, for there
is a big difference between what happens as a result of something else
and what merely happens after it.'[50] 'Probable' has two senses here:
it means, on the one hand, natural, life-like, and, on the other, cohe-
sive, logical, and the latter is supposed to guarantee the former –
causal coherence is an attribute of nature. Such a reading of the
dramatic process unduly privileges one dimension of the theatrical
medium (the dimension of linear time-flow) against another (the
principle of simultaneity) whereby the meaning of every utterance or
gesture on the stage is conditioned by the actual presence of its
addressee, who may explicitly through speech, or implicitly through
silence, contest its validity or definitiveness.

The privileging of *plot* (an abstract notion which bears no relation to physical actions on the stage) seeks to find in the demonstrable causes and ultimate *resolution* of events an authoritative perspective on what is potentially a polyphonic medium, where competing perspectives are not subject to any single higher or unifying perspective. Carnivalesque performance, on the other hand, strives to free itself from all finalising authority, even the authority of time. Hence its key principles of construction are those described by Artaud as quintessentially theatrical rather than literary – 'the combination, interaction, and mutual subversion of all its elements' ('mimicry, gesture, dance, voice', etc.).[51] Carnivalesque plays bring the aim of generating a saturated, simultaneous and sensory experience where opposites co-exist, collide, or interrupt each other into a problematic relationship with the aim of narrating a series of events with a beginning, a middle and an end.

Bottom's 'dream', for example, where the mechanical sleeps with the fairy queen, enacts the intersection of all the play's opposing conceptual categories (high, low; supernatural, natural; human, animal; rational, irrational) but is pointedly not reassimilated into the linear, narrative order. 'The eye of man hath not heard, man's hand is not able to taste, his tongue to conceive, nor his heart to report, what my dream was. I will get Peter Quince to write a ballad of this dream. It shall be call'd "Bottom's Dream", because it hath no bottom; and I will sing it in the latter end of a play, before the Duke' (*A Midsummer Night's Dream*, iv.i.214–19). The attempt to verbalise the experience progressively falsifies it, and in this failure invokes the disjunction between the simultaneous and sensory world of theatre, where sight, speech, hearing and even touch are interfused, and the progressively more abstract and stabilised worlds of speech 'dream' is already an inadequate description) and literature ('I will get Peter Quince to write . . .'). In the contrast between bottomlessness (infinity) and ends (teleology), the point is made that the formal conclusion will in no sense contain or resolve the reversal. Nor in the event will Bottom make any attempt to describe his experience to Duke Theseus, the play's representative of social authority, and at one point its spokesman for reason against fancy. Endings repress the utopian and anarchic complexity of reversals.

Measure for Measure is, to my mind, both Shakespeare's most consistently carnivalesque play and the one which illustrates most clearly the carnivalesque hostility to narrative order.[52] By investing three kinds of authority – theological, political, and authorial or dramaturgical – in a single figure, who is little more than a blood-less and discontinuous series of roles, the play contrives, brilliantly, to subvert from within everything that is potentially authoritarian in dramatic 'plots'. The authority of the shadowy Duke, whom Lucio calls 'the old fantastical duke of dark corners' (iv.iii.1152–3), over the anarchic play which he frames, is persistently thrown into question by the anti-hierarchical and anti-teleological means of saturated stage images, ironical scenic juxtapositions, puns, re-versals and doublings. The Duke, in disguise as a monk, having temporarily abdicated his throne to his deputy, wanders through his kingdom castigating immorality, comforting the afflicted, making moralising asides to the audience about corruption and imposture, and working in secret to avert the disastrous consequences of his deputy's revealed ruthlessness. Finally he restores order to the king-dom by publicly exposing the deputy's criminality while triumphantly demonstrating his own capacity for Christian clemency in forgiving him.

This is one kind of summary of what goes on, and it has led some critics (notably Wilson Knight) to propose that the Duke is an alle-gory of the Incarnate Lord or Providence.[53] But in performance we can more easily see the play as the occasion for bizarre, carnivalesque confrontations of apparently opposing worlds and their idiom – court, prison, nunnery, brothel – which adumbrate the social and psycho-logical dialectic summed up in one of Blake's aphorisms: 'Prisons are built with stones of law, Brothels with bricks of religion'. Fur-thermore, the sequential plot itself has carnivalesque connotations, since it proceeds downwards from court to prison by punning on the idea of *substitution*, and hence suggests a kind of grotesque masquer-ade in which everybody successively takes on another's role, thus undermining all claims to social and moral distinction. It begins with an official act of substitution when the Duke mysteriously deputes his authority to Angelo, an action which comes to seem morally dubious when the Duke all but says to the Friar that it has enabled him to split his need to be popular from the necessary harshness of his public role (i.iii.40–3). Angelo is disliked anyway, so he can enforce the Duke's more unpleasant moral aspirations.

Subsequently the theme of substitution is transposed into a lower key, when the *pro*-stitution of Mariana for Isabella in the bed-trick (also instigated by the Duke) enables the nun to avoid choosing between her obligations as a natural and religious sister, but only at the price of splitting herself into two and surrogating the natural part

– affection, sexuality, sullied reputation – to poor Mariana. Finally the Duke seeks to avert the inhuman consequences of an inhuman law (which he after all asked Angelo to enforce) by the last-minute substitution of an inhuman (social-outcast) victim for a human one (i.e. one who had 'a most noble father' – II.i.7).

This progression, through evasion, implies the viciousness of the chain of command: the Duke is God's substitute on earth, but like God he himself absconds. Angelo does the Duke's dirty work for him and so on down the chain of command to the pimp and executioner. But it also carnivalises this hierarchy by making the disguised Duke become an intimate party to the very activities which he rails at: in instigating the bed-trick he becomes a pimp; in discussing ways of disfiguring corpses for the highest moral purposes he reveals a morbid glee no less distasteful than his deputy's more obvious savagery; and finally, by quite unexpectedly asking the nun Isabella to marry him in the last lines of the play, he shows that his acts of charity towards suffering women have not been untouched by eros. (The script, incidentally, leaves the nun's reaction to this astonishing proposal to the actress.) All of these possible duplicities of ducal motive are hinted at by the clowning nonsense of Pompey Bum (the name itself is a marvellous debasement of greatness) and the slanders of the whoremaster Lucio (III.ii). It is presumably because the pimp–executioner and the whoremaster are such unflattering doubles of himself that the Duke flies into a rage against Pompey's 'stink' (III.ii.24) and forgets his role of Mercy in his disproportionately vicious sentence on Lucio in the last scene.

The point at which the principle of providential plot – with the Duke as *deus ex machina* – and that of carnivalesque confrontation climactically intersect is in Act IV, scene iii. Pompey Bum, who is often simply called Clown in the script, has accepted the occupation of executioner to gain remission from a prison sentence for pimping. He now stands next to Abhorson, the official executioner. Together they drag Barnardine, a drunken criminal who has suddenly been produced to fulfil the demands of the plot, when a head is needed, to the chopping-block. The Duke approaches in his monkish disguise offering to confess the prisoner whose execution he has just engineered. Political power wears the mask of religion. But, in response, Barnardine simply roars out, 'I swear I will not die today for any man's persuasion!' (IV.iii.56). The hybrid carnival image of sex and death (clown–pimp and executioner) in levelling partnership is used to parody moral allegory. Pompey is Carnal Folly sharpening the axe

of sin by which Mankind (Barnardine) will die eternally, and prat-
tling jokes to distract him from Salvation. Abhorson in black costume
and mask is Death: his name plays between a reference to Death as
the son of a whore (Sin) and the injunction to abhor sin. In contrast
to Carnal Folly, Death prompts Mankind to seek salvation: 'Truly,
sir, I would desire you to clap into your prayers' (IV.iii.38–39). Now
a shadowy cowled figure approaches, whom Abhorson announces as
'your ghostly father' (IV.iv.44–5). This is surely God. But awesome
allegory is invoked only to be dissolved in laughter when Barnardine
exits back to his straw more like an animal than an immortal soul:
'Not a word; if you have anything to say to me, come to my ward'
(IV.iii.58–9). After Barnardine's abrupt exit, the Folio gives a line to
the Duke – 'After him fellows; bring him to the block.' (IV.iii.61) –
which the Arden editor, following Dr Johnson, gives to the Provost
because it is too undignified to pass ducal lips. But I believe that the
bathos (present anyway in Barnardine's reaction) is intended. As
Barnardine usurps the role of Authority, so the Duke loses his com-
posure.

The Duke's sudden panic is quite in keeping with the incongruous
effect made by the speech in which he has just planned Barnardine's
death, where pastoral and biblical cadences of great beauty give way
to routine brutality: 'Look, th' unfolding star calls up the shepherd.
Put not yourself into amazement how these things should be; all
difficulties are but easy when they are known. Call your executioner
and off with Barnardine's head' (IV.ii.194–8). The role of sublime
moralist, and that of plot, are incongruous partners, and it is precisely
this incongruity which Shakespeare is aiming at by the almost inde-
cent haste of the last two acts, which critics have objected to because
'the plot goes thin'.[54] What happens, I think, is that the scapegoat
structure which has been implicit in the plots of most Shakespearian
comedies (Shylock, Falstaff, Malvolio) is brought to light and sub-
verted. This time the scapegoat refuses to accept his appointed role
and it is the ritual pattern that requires scapegoats which is made to
look ridiculous. Beyond artistic self-parody, there is the very serious
point that all religions which seek to justify suffering as part of a
divine plan become themselves cruel.

Shakespeare is to reassert the motif of festive levelling in the
judgement scene at the end of the play, when, quite counter to the
requirements of probability, he has Barnardine, a minor character
who only appears momentarily, brought back onto the stage to participate in the conclusion. Again he forms part of a grotesque visual

trio: Claudio with his head 'muffled' (blind love), Juliet pregnant (natural fecundity) and Barnardine (unaccommodated man). The Duke appears on paper to have the last word, but his speech also suggests what the Arden editor describes as a subsequent processional exit in pairs, led by the Duke and Isabella and ending with Friar Peter and Barnardine, and Lucio under guard. No exit of so many people would be effective if they went directly through one of the two available doors at the back of the stage. So the 'procession' has to wind round the stage. In doing so it gives plenty of scope for farcical business as the audience applauds.

Some suggestions for performance: the Duke woos Isabella with increasing ardour, but she continues to resist; Lucio, garrulous as ever, is protesting his fate; and finally the head of the procession gets mixed up with its tail, and goes on circling. In short, no ending at all but increasing muddle. Such theatrical relativising of language by gesture, hierarchy by levelling, speech by action, ending by continuing, is quite compatible with the whole tone of the play. The potential for this kind of stage business has already been established in Act II, where a parodic court scene leads to the malapropistic constable Elbow (another joke on the Body Politic) misunderstanding the verdict: 'Thou seest, thou wicked varlet, what's come upon thee: thou art to continue, now, thou varlet, thou art to continue' (II.i.181–3). There follows a serious court scene between Angelo and Isabella, which is ironised by a visual parody of the Good and Bad Angel convention from the morality–play tradition, with the Provost on one side of the stage as Good Angel, with his eyes raised to heaven ('Heaven give thee moving graces!' – (II.ii.37) while Lucio, as Bad Angel, offers sexual advice to the nun as to how to move the Justice: 'Kneel down before him, hang upon his gown'; 'You are too cold'; 'Aye, touch him' (II.ii.44, 56, 70). The irony is that the spokesman for Providence and the spokesman for the flesh are both offering the same advice. Both offer different frameworks for describing the same ambivalent world and its irrational origins.

The play has for the last fifty years been regarded as a 'problem play', but it is only a problem to those who have seen it as aiming at Aristotelian consistency and Christian morality. In those terms it fails. Regarded as a thoroughly theatrical celebration of carnivalesque dialectics and paradox, it is not only one of Shakespeare's most complete successes, but also – to transpose Shklovsky's tribute to the apparent chaos of Sterne's parodic novel, *Tristram Shandy* – the most typical play in world theatre.[55]

Georg Büchner's *Woyzeck*: 'reason' turned inside-out

In seventeenth-century England, Puritan hostility to popular festivity and to theatre disrupted the festive tradition which had reached its pinnacle of achievement with Shakespeare and Jonson. After the Restoration, an essentially bourgeois, classicising literary milieu which prided itself on its separation from the vulgar, the irrational and the barbaric discouraged the interplay of extreme opposites – stylistic, social and metaphysical – upon which carnivalesque aesthetics depend. The Fool was excised from performances of *King Lear* because his painful and often sexual jesting threatened the tragic dignity of the suffering king. Carnivalesque logic, banished from the theatres, nevertheless persisted in the theatrical novels of Swift, Fielding, Sterne and Diderot, which owe much to the Erasmian–Rabelaisian tradition of paradoxical 'folly'. It was not until German Romanticism that there was a significant revival of the carnivalesque impulse in the theatre ('the return of Hans Wurst to the stage'[56]), one which was notably inspired by Shakespeare's and Sterne's resistance to Aristotelian precepts. The practice of Georg Büchner is particularly important in this context, because, besides admiring Shakespeare's freedom from moral and aesthetic prejudice, he also looked directly to popular art forms – puppet shows, ballads, fairgrounds, fairy tales – to provide formal vehicles for challenging the ideological perspectives of 'high' art. In *Danton's Death* the grotesque dance of death becomes for the first time an explicit image of revolution, and the puppet show of the impotence of the individual to alter history.[57] But once again ambivalence dogs the images of reversal. Just as overtly theological plays, such as *Mankind*, have a covert political dimension, so it is the metaphysical implications of reversal which attract Büchner the revolutionary.

Woyzeck (1835–6), often hailed as the first proletarian tragedy and not performed until the twentieth century, is clearly designed to upset a bourgeois audience's generic expectations. The peasant batman Woyzeck has a Hamlet-like gift for metaphysical speculation and a tragic destiny, while the ruling-class figures, the Captain and the Doctor (the first a fat repressed sensualist, the second a thin sadist), are conceived of as a pair of comic grotesques. Each of the drastically compressed scenes centres on a reversal of mood, and they are juxtaposed one against the other, with little regard for narrative sequence, to convey a sense of kaleidoscopic change and ambiguity. This breaks down any Aristotelian continuity of plot, so that, for example, at one moment we are outside a fairground booth, and at the next, inside it. The fairground scene (scene iii) centres on the patter of a showman who displays, in typically carnivalesque style, a monkey dressed as a soldier, and a horse who can do arithmetic and is honoured as 'a member of all learned societies and a professor at the university'.[58] (Animals are parodically honoured; rational man is debased.) But, just when the peasant crowd is giggling and marvelling at the horse's 'inside-out thinking' (*doppelte Raison*), the horse defecates, and the jovial showman rounds on the audience: 'You were fashioned out of dust, out of sand, out of mud – would you be anything more than dust, sand and mud' (p. 8). Carnival has turned abruptly into Lent, as the showman preaches a miniature funeral sermon.

In a similar rapid series of reversals in scene xii, an anarchically pagan spectacle of dancing – where the partners perpetually swop as if in mockery of marriage, and two journeymen sing drinking-songs – suddenly changes tone when Woyzeck blasphemes and interprets the festive tavern scene as apocalyptic: 'Why don't you blow the sun out, God? Let everything fall over itself in its lewdness. Flesh, filth, man, woman, animal' (p. 25). Then one of the journeymen stands on the table to preach a sermon which seems at first to express a drunken upsurge of religious sentiment ('Brethren – think now upon the Wanderer, who stands beside the stream of time and communes with himself, receiving the wisdom of god and saying, "Wherefore is man?" And again, "Wherefore is man?"'), but gradually reveals itself to be a jeering parody ('How should the tailor ply his trade if God had not implanted shame in the human breast? Or the soldier his, if man had not been equipped with the need for self-destruction?'), and ends with outright blasphemy ('So in conclusion, beloved – let's piss on the crucifix and a Jew will die!' – p. 25). Büchner is preoccupied with the coexistence of scriptural and carnivalesque idiom among the Hessian peasantry. This is nowhere clearer than in the first scene between Woyzeck and the Doctor (scene vi) where the immemorial peasant idiom, oscillating between materialism and mysticism, confronts and baffles the bourgeois language of science and reason. The Doctor is infuriated by Woyzeck's failure to deliver a sample of urine: he is feeding him solely on a diet of peas. 'Haven't I demonstrated that the *musculus constricta vesicae* is subject to the will? – Nature! Man is free, Woyzeck. Man is the ultimate expression of the individual urge to freedom!' (p. 13). But the peasant, who simply had to piss against the wall, turns philosopher in reply: 'D'you see,

Doctor? A man might have one sort of character, one sort of make-up – nature's something again: nature's a thing – *flicks his finger to catch it*.' Thus the argument between Kantian moral voluntarism and materialist determinism is judged in favour of determinism via a parodic philosophical debate about pissing (the grotesque canon). A second and quite distinct challenge to bourgeois 'reason' lies in store, as the peasant switches his ground. 'Doctor,' asks Woyzeck with disarming confidentiality, 'have you ever seen nature inside-out [*doppelte Natur*]?' The phrase *doppelte Natur* echoes the showman's *doppelte Raison*.

> WOYZECK. Have you ever seen nature inside-out Doctor? When the sun stands still at midday and it's as if the world was going up in flames? That's when a terrible voice spoke to me.
> DOCTOR. You've an aberration, Woyzeck.
> WOYZECK. Yes, nature, Doctor, when nature's out?
> DOCTOR. What does that mean 'when nature's out'?
> WOYZECK. When nature's out, that's – when nature's out. When the world gets so dark you have to feel your way round with your hands, till you think it's coming apart like a spider's web.
>
> (p. 14)

Woyzeck's language here, as elsewhere in the play, recalls the cosmic reversal of biblical apocalypse (e.g. Revelation 21:3; 2 Peter 3). But in inhabiting that idiom he is also struggling to articulate a quite personal experience of the omnipresence of death as a natural fact which threatens at every moment to reverse our common-sense perceptions of what is real or substantial. The darkness, the feeling with hands, the spider's web suggest a mode of consciousness ungoverned by the rational constructions of causality, substance and identity. Thus the peasant's language struggles to hold in a single moment the involuntary experience of instinct – birth, nature, urination – and the consciousness of death which alienates man from nature, and turns nature 'inside-out'. But this experience of extreme natural contradiction and of human heteronomy is also the prelude to a mystical experience in which the silence of nature is perceived as identical with the voice of God. The Doctor's 'reason' – his illusion of man's capacity to control nature and do without God – is shown to be no more than a fantastic organisation of the world around the human ego. In Woyzeck he confronts an image of his own true condition, which he must metaphorically bind and kill, to sustain his own illusion of power.

Büchner is in two minds about the peasant experience of heteronomy – of being a mere puppet, or a broken spider's web. On the one hand, like Marx, he is outraged by the bourgeois appropriation of working-class labour, and calls for revolution: this is one meaning of the apocalypse, the reversal of 'natural' order, which Woyzeck glimpses. On the other hand, he perceives how the experience of slavery, and of the pulls of nature and civilisation as contradiction, is the necessary condition of mystical experience. It is no accident that Woyzeck gravitates to what is Saturnalian, antinomian and apocalyptic in the Bible, while the Captain, ignorant of scripture, treats Christianity as a closed system of moral and social values superintended by the Church.

> CAPTAIN. Morals are well observing morality, you understand. You've got a child without the church's blessing as our reverend padre calls it . . .
> WOYZECK. Sir, God the Father isn't going to worry if nobody said amen at the poor worm's making. The Lord said, 'suffer little children to come unto me'. (pp. 11–12)

At this moment Woyzeck *is* Christ opposing the Pharisees (though 'worm' lets in nihilism), while in another scene Marie, who prays to the guileless Christ while protesting her inability to 'sin no more', is both nature contesting theology and an image of Mary Magdalen, to whom much is forgiven because she loves much (p. 29). Even the blasphemous journeyman performs an ambivalent ritual for the audience, in simultaneously breaking down the ruling-class image of God as tyranny writ large, and betraying, in the vestigial beauty of the cadence which he deforms, the yearning of the spirit. Thus Büchner is determined to do justice to the peasants' consciousness, their language, their songs, their fairground and tavern parodies, which transform the moral frameworks which are imposed upon them by Church, state and 'science', so as to express a vision which embraces materialism, nihilism and mysticism in a paradoxical unity. That is why attempts to produce the play as naturalistic theatre about a peasant Othello driven to murder by sexual jealousy and maddened by a diet of peas are so misguided: they work inside the Doctor's world picture, which sees Woyzeck as an interesting aberration whose behaviour can be scientifically explained. Rather the play – in being thoroughly carnivalesque in its form – takes the side of the peasantry. Its performance must upset the audience's own sense of a causally coherent and intelligible world. It is not Woyzeck who is on trial, but trials themselves that are.

Postscript

I must leave the reader to decide how strained it would be to apply the terms that I have advanced to contemporary theatre. On the one hand, there are no longer significant links between popular festivities (which no longer exist) and theatre (which is no longer popular). On the other hand, there are important analogies to be drawn between pre-individualist and post-individualist theatre. Perhaps as a response to the commercial mass-production networks into which individual lives are organised, and to the threat of collective extinction in international wars, a sense of the self as a provisional locus of relationships and roles rather than a stable entity has become widespread. This new kind of awareness has been underpinned by the epistemological reorientations initiated by Marx, Freud and Saussure. The sense of the dependence of constructed, dialogic and fluctuating subjects upon impersonal cultural systems is reflected in plays where the grammatical or social system rather than the individual character is the object of investigation (e.g. Beckett, Genet, Brecht). In this context role-reversals and parodies take on a renewed importance. They become dialectical devices for undermining the centrality of the individual ego while also relativising the impersonal systems of organisation which repress variety and innovation. They negate an outmoded form of humanism while refusing to capitulate to its destructive alternative – a dehumanising determinism in which subjectivity has no place.

NOTES

1.   Francis Bacon, *Works* (London, 1824) p. 489.
2.   M. Gluckman, 'On Drama, Games and Athletic Contests', in S. F. Moore and B. G. Myerhoff (eds), *Secular Ritual* (Assen and Amsterdam, 1977). The rest of this paragraph is based on Max Gluckman, *Custom and Conflict in Africa* (Oxford, 1956).
3.   K. Thomas, 'Rule and Misrule in the Schools of Early Modern England', Stenton Lecture, Reading, 1976; C. Phythian-Adams, 'Cer-

emony and the Citizen: The Communal Year at Coventry', in P. Clark (ed.), *The Early Modern Town* (London, 1976).

4. N. Z. Davis, *Society and Culture in Early Modern France* (London, 1975) p. 119.
5. Quoted in A. H. Nelson, *The Medieval Stage* (Chicago, 1974) p. 123.
6. Davis, *Society and Culture*, p. 119.
7. E. Le Roy Ladurie, *Carnival in Romans*, trs. M. Feeney (New York, 1979) p. xvi.
8. Davis, *Society and Culture*, p. 148; and U. Henriques, 'Bastardy and the New Poor Law', *Past and Present*, 87 (1980) 98–127.
9. Mikhail Bakhtin, *Rabelais and his World*, trs. H. Iswolsky (Cambridge, Mass., 1968) p. 11.
10. Mikhail Bakhtin, *Problems of Dostoyevsky's Poetics*, trs. R. W. Rotsel (1973) p. 103.
11. Ibid., p. 101.
12. Ibid., p. 160.
13. Bakhtin, *Rabelais and his World*, p. 83.
14. Ibid., pp. 18–34 and *passim*.
15. Ibid., p. 19.
16. Peter Stallybrass and Allon White, *The Politics and Poetics of Transgression* (London, 1986) pp. 6–26.
17. M. A. Screech, *Rabelais* (London, 1979) p. 51.
18. For treatments of the relation between popular culture and theatre in the Renaissance period, see Robert Weimann, *Shakespeare and the Popular Tradition in the Theater* (Baltimore, 1978); and Michael P. Bristol, *Carnival and Theatre: Plebeian Culture and the Structure of Authority in Renaissance England* (New York and London, 1984).
19. Peter Burke, *Popular Culture in Early Modern Europe* (London, 1978) p. 200.
20. C. L. Barber, *Shakespeare's Festive Comedy*, 2nd edn (Princeton, NJ, 1972) p. 205; cf. p. 102, below. Donaldson cites Gluckman on the strengthening and preservation of hierarchy by reversal: I. Donaldson, *The World Upside-Down* (Oxford, 1979) pp. 14–15; cf. p. 102, below.
21. Leonard Tennenhouse, *Power on Display: The Politics of Shakespeare's Genres* (New York and London, 1986) p. 89.
22. William Empson, *Some Versions of Pastoral* (London, 1935); A. P. Rossiter, *English Drama from Early Times to the Elizabethans* (London, 1950) and *Angel with Horns* (London, 1961).
23. William Empson, *Some Versions of Pastoral*, Peregrine edn (Harmondsworth, Middx, 1966) p. 58.
24. Barber, *Shakespeare's Festive Comedy*, pp. 6–15.
25. K. Marx and F. Engels, 'The German Ideology', *Collected Works*, v (London, 1976) p. 36. For fuller discussion of images of inversion in Marx and Engels, see Frederic Jameson, *Marxism and Form* (Princeton, NJ, 1974) pp. 369–72.
26. Aeschylus, *Agamemnon*, ll. 1384–92, quoted and discussed in John Jones, *On Aristotle and Greek Tragedy* (London, 1968) pp. 120–1.

27. See Stuart Clark, 'Inversion, Misrule and the Meaning of Witchcraft', *Past and Present*, 37 (1967) 103–29.
28. Plato, *The Republic*, VII, 518c.
29. Erasmus, *In Praise of Folly*, trs. Betty Radice (Harmondsworth, Middx, 1971) p. 103.
30. Edmund Leach, 'Two Essays Concerning the Symbolic Representation of Time', *Rethinking Anthropology* (London, 1966) p. 136.
31. Friedrich Nietzsche, *The Birth of Tragedy*, trs. F. Golffing (New York, 1956) p. 27.
32. F. H. Sandbach, *The Comic Theatre of Greece and Rome* (London, 1977) p. 34.
33. Francis Cornford, *The Origin of Attic Comedy*, ed. T. H. Gaster (New York, 1961).
34. All quotations from *Lysistrata* are from Aristophanes, *Plays 2*, trs. P. Dickinson (London, 1970). Page references relate to this edition.
35. Victor Turner, *The Ritual Process* (Harmondsworth, Middx, 1969).
36. See ibid., pp. 172–4.
37. On Aristophanes' politics, from a Marxist perspective, see G. E. M. de Ste Croix, *The Origins of the Peloponnesian War* (London, 1972) pp. 351–71.
38. O. B. Hardison, *Christian Rite and Christian Drama in the Middle Ages* (Baltimore, 1969) p. 285.
39. For a fuller discussion of the play's festive background see A. Gash, 'Carnival against Lent: The Ambivalence of Medieval Drama', in D. Aers (ed.), *Medieval Literature* (Brighton, 1986) pp. 74–99.
40. Quotations from *Mankind* are from *The Macro Plays*, ed. Mark Eccles, Early English Text Society, OS 262 (Oxford, 1969).
41. Aristotle, 'The Poetics', in *Classical Literary Criticism*, trs. T. S. Dorsch (Harmondsworth, Middx, 1965) p. 51.
42. Ibid., p. 41.
43. Barber, *Shakespeare's Festive Comedy*, p. 245.
44. Shakespeare quotations are from Shakespeare, *The Complete Works*, ed. P. Alexander (London and Glasgow, 1951). Line references relate to this edition.
45. For an extension of this suggestion to the 'play-boy' in general, see Lisa Jardine, 'Female Roles and Elizabethan Eroticism', *Still Harping on Daughters* (Brighton, 1983) pp. 9–36.
46. Plato, *Phaedrus*, 250c.
47. Plato, *Symposium*, 189e–193d.
48. Bakhtin, *Problems of Dostoyevsky's Poetics*, p. 102.
49. This episode is discussed in similar terms by Neil Rhodes in *Elizabethan Grotesque* (London, 1983) p. 117.
50. Aristotle, in *Classical Literary Criticism*, p. 45.
51. Antonin Artaud, *The Theatre and its Double*, trs. V. Corti (London, 1974) p. 28.
52. Jonathan Dollimore's 'Transgression and Surveillance in *Measure for Measure*', in J. Dollimore and A. Sinfield (eds), *Political Shakespeare: New Essays in Cultural Materialism* (Manchester, 1985) pp. 72–87, tries to forestall a carnivalesque reading of *Measure for Meas-*

ure, but is taken to task by Charles Swann in 'Lucio: Benefactor or Malefactor?', *Critical Quarterly*, 29, no. 1 (1985) 55–70, for not giving any weight to the presence and voice of Lucio in the last act.

53. G. Wilson Knight, *The Wheel of Fire* (London, 1930).
54. For instance Rossiter, *Angel with Horns*, p. 169.
55. Victor Shklovsky, 'Sterne's *Tristram Shandy*', in L. T. Lemon and M. J. Reis (eds), *Russian Formalistic Criticism* (Lincoln, Nebr., 1965).
56. For an outline discussion of this development see J. Hilton, *Georg Büchner* (London, 1982) ch. 2.
57. 'We are puppets, pulled on strings by unknown forces; nothing, we ourselves are nothing' (*Danton's Death*, II.v). In a letter of 1834 Büchner wrote, 'The individual is merely foam on a wave, greatness mere accident, the rule of genius is puppetry, a ridiculous wrestling with an iron law in which the greatest achievement is simply to become aware of it' (quoted in Hilton, *Georg Büchner*, p. 87).
58. Quotations are from Georg Büchner, *Woyzeck*, trs. John Mackendrick (London, 1979). Page references relate to this edition.

Chapter 6

The Hermeneutic Approach to Theatre and Drama

ELINOR SHAFFER

'Hermeneutics', or the art of interpretation, today more precisely the theory of interpretative methods in the humanities and social sciences, has emerged as one of the most stimulating and productive of several new directions in recent criticism. It is hardly a complete newcomer: traditionally associated with techniques of exegesis or explanation of individual passages of the Bible and the classics, it has since the late eighteenth century been increasingly applied to a wide range of texts. One of the steps in this direction was the perception that the Bible was not a uniquely inspired or revealed text, but itself literary in character; thus techniques for explicating the Bible became fully available for explicating literary texts generally, and these techniques in turn underwent a sea-change as what we would now call 'literary criticism' began to be formulated and practised.

Hermeneutics was reformulated as a general theory in the early nineteenth century, and came to be seen as the key to understanding not only literature but the whole range of the humanities and the 'human sciences'. A fierce debate over whether the new knowledge about mankind gathered by the study of comparative religion and mythology, anthropology and sociology was appropriately understood as 'science' on the model of the natural sciences led to the emergence of hermeneutics as the method of the human sciences as distinguished from the method of the natural sciences.

In the twentieth century, philosophy, anthropology, psychology, psychoanalysis, and communication theory have continued to develop and refine hermeneutic method. One of the most stimulating aspects of this development is that is makes the whole range of modern social science available to the theatre.

While much has been written about the relation of hermeneutics to poetics, poetry and fiction, little has been done in English to elucidate dramatic texts and performance from a hermeneutic point of view. This is surprising, for hermeneutics has had a close link with drama throughout the history of its modern, secular development, from the late eighteenth century to the present.

The origins of hermeneutics

To understand the developing functions of hermeneutics, we must briefly trace its history back to the centres of classical Western culture. The Athenians of the fifth century BC revered the epics of Homer, the *Iliad* and the *Odyssey*, but had to labour to extricate their literal sense: not only were they already several centuries old, but Homeric Greek is a specialised bardic language that combines elements of several dialects. Hermeneutics, then, is in the first instance the discipline that permits the clarification of obscurities and distortions that arise through the aging of a statement made in the past, and ensures the preservation of the text despite changes in language and attitudes. The hermeneutic art was never limited to the determination of the literal meaning of the text. It aims at reintegrating a sacred, canonical or centrally significant text into the present time, at reformulating it so that it can still be seen as valid by a new generation. In short, its task at all times is the modernisation of existing interpretation.

The Alexandrian school of Hellenistic and Judaic exegesis in the first century AD began the allegorical interpretation of the Homeric books and the technique of 'figural' interpretation. Allegory, as applied especially by Origin to Christian ends, developed into one of the most powerful techniques for reinterpretation. A brilliant example, illustrating the boldness with which the technique was often applied, is Bernard of Clairvaux's twelfth-century allegorical interpretation of the *Song of Songs*, whereby that erotic poem is transformed into a celebration of the marriage of the Church to its bridegroom, Christ. According to figural or typological interpretation, the Old Testament is a foreshadowing and even a prophecy of the events of the New. Thus the two Testaments of the Bible, widely separated in time, ethos and language, were drawn together. Through the work of St Augustine, Gregory the Great and a succession of monastic and scholastic schools, a fourfold method of interpretation was developed, which flourished from medieval times to the seventeenth century. Each of the four levels (the literal, the moral, the allegorical, and the anagogical or spiritual) was explicated in turn, and the interpretation at each level was considered indispensable and correct in itself; but the meaning of the text as a whole could only be fully understood through the completed fourfold interpretation. The bold work of interpretation was crowned in the case of the Bible by the still more audacious claim that the text as a whole was divinely inspired.

One of the monumental achievements of hermeneutics was to salvage a large portion of the corpus of classical writing and integrate it into the alien Christian context. Radical methods of interpretation were required to reconcile the apparently irreconcilable modes of pagan and Christian. Many of the techniques we now think of as literary criticism were forged under this pressure.

Into the Enlightenment

The new pressures of scientific rationalism and the drive to political egalitarianism led in the eighteenth century to new techniques of interpretation of the Bible which carried the critical arts into the arena of public, secular controversy. The attack on the unity, authenticity and inspiration of the Bible was a major priority of the Enlightenment. What was seen as a conspiracy of despotism and priestcraft to keep the people in subjection had to be unmasked. The Reformation had put the text within reach of everyone; now the institutional veils needed to be torn away.

Historical questions were asked of the text so long hedged about with assumptions of its divine authorship, and historical questioning gradually became a vital part of the new hermeneutics. If the Bible was not literally the 'word of God', who had written it? When, and in what circumstances, and for what purposes had it been written? What validity could be attached to its reports of miraculous events? The searching inquiry was carried on with all the resources of theological and philosophical polemic, with the weapons of literary satire, irony, lampoon, and parody, and with the sober, probing factual style of the new empiricism. New styles of hermeneutic analysis were cultivated by Spinoza, the English Deists, and the French *philosophes*.

Historical inquiry into a text hitherto considered fixed for all time lent itself to the development of historicism, or the reading of the meaning of events through their historical unfolding rather than through their timeless significance. Giambattista Vico, in the *New Science* (1725), grasped the essential point that history is not merely about events and their succession, but also about men's experience and their understanding of it. Shifts in awareness over time became a subject for investigation in themselves. 'Change' rather than 'permanence' captured the interest of the period.

Here we begin to see the emergence of one of the salient characteristics of modern hermeneutics: the extension of the meaning of 'text'. To establish the facts about past events might be troublesome enough, but to grasp the nature of the milieu in which they took place, and the principles, motives and emotional make-up of the actors – all part of the wider 'text' – could require an enormous investment of energy.

J. G. Herder (1744–1803), a leading figure of the German Enlightenment, coined a phrase for the understanding of historical change from within: *Einfühlung*, or empathy. This conception had a far-reaching significance for the theory and practice of interpretation, and for the creation of new works of every kind, not least drama. Herder addressed himself to drama directly, especially in his brilliant essay of 1770 on Shakespeare, in which he suggested that *King Lear*, like each of Shakespeare's plays, represented a whole dramatic world in which everything was essential and interconnected. this heralded a revolution. At that time, Shakespeare was always played in cut versions and in adaptations, even in England, and the translations into French and German reflect the view that the barbarous Shakespeare called for through revision. Herder offered a hermeneutic justification for what was to be a long process of restoration of the full texts of the plays, for reading and for acting. Furthermore, the notion of the 'world' within which the spectator must learn to feel at home made the technique of empathy essential to the understanding of individual works of art.

In his major contribution to the new movement in biblical criticism, *The Spirit of Hebrew Poetry* (1782), he carried further the principle that the whole historical milieu must be reconstructed if the Bible were to be made comprehensible to modern readers. Only in this way could the 'primitive' folk poetry of the Bible – like the 'primitive' poetry of Shakespeare – be appreciated by a sophisticated contemporary audience, and lead to a renewal of literature itself.

In his *Ideas* he proposed a comprehensive account of the organic development of civilisations, each of which has its period of growth, decay and death, but whose achievements are permanent acquisitions of the human race. Herder's approach not only led to an evolutionary theory of culture, but also suggested the hermeneutic reading of a cultural world as a 'text' with a significance attaching to the whole.

Friedrich Schleiermacher and the founding of modern hermeneutics

Friedrich Schleiermacher (1768–1834) gave hermeneutics a decisive new turn. His 'general hermeneutics' laid the groundwork for the modern development of the method. Primarily a religious philosopher (Dilthey was to call him 'the greatest German theologian since Luther'), Schleiermacher was cast in a new mould. He was closely associated with the group of young writers who initiated the German Romantic movement in the 1790s, and who included among their number the translator of Shakespeare A. W. Schlegel, and Ludwig Tieck, a major playwright whose innovations have still to be fully registered in the English-speaking world. Schleiermacher's first book, *Discourses on Religion* (1799), signalled the appearance of a new form of religious apprehension in a new style.

Schleiermacher undertook the translation of all of Plato's dialogues, and his is still the standard translation of Plato in German. His introductions to the individual dialogue exemplified the new hermeneutic approach. He attempted to establish the authenticity and inner structure of the dialogues, and the relations between them, in accordance with his deepening conception, which progressed as he proceeded through the dialogues, of the significance of Platonic philosophy as a whole. This reciprocal movement from the parts to the whole and back again is a version of what became known as 'the hermeneutic circle'. His exploration of the dialogue form is itself a contribution to dramatic theory, and was instrumental in the formulation of a new dialectics; in Hegel's *Lectures on Aesthetics* drama would take pride of place as the synthesis of the antithetical genres epic and lyric. Schleiermacher's essay 'On Translation' marks a turning-point in the theory of translation, for 'translation' is presented as a fundamental element in all understanding and communication, even within the same language.

The process of understanding lies at the centre of Schleiermacher's hermeneutics. In order to understand any text whatever, the audience must relive an alien experience. It must follow and undergo the experience of the author who created the text, itself an imaginative reconstruction. Schleiermacher borrowed from and reinforced the Romantic stress on the creative process of the imagination, both in the author and in the audience. In the case of the anonymous author and an unknown audience (as with the Bible and Homer), the techniques of the 'higher criticism' could be used to reconstruct and make accessible the historical milieu which was the locus of the alien experience.

The meaning of the text shifted with each successive community that received it. Successive reconstructions would be required. Herder's notion of 'empathy' was refined and problematised. To this complex process of reconstruction Schleiermacher gave the name *Verstehen* ('understanding'). This became a key term in subsequent debates over the contrast between 'explanation' in the natural sciences and 'understanding' in the human sciences; by the end of the century, it had been defined as the method of the human sciences by Wilhelm Dilthey and Max Weber. The stress on the active role of the interpretative community or audience became a major tenet of hermeneutics.

The hermeneutic analysis thus became applicable to all acts of understanding. The imagination must place itself within the experience of another, who might or might not be far removed in place and time. Even one's own experience might become alien and need to be recaptured or replayed. Any attempt to understand the past, or another's experience, had to overcome fragmentation and a sense of alienation. The crisis of the text became general. The nature and possibility of communication itself was at stake.

Wilhelm Dilthey and twentieth-century hermeneutics

Wilhelm Dilthey (1833–1911), although primarily a philosopher of the historical and social sciences, was also a literary critic who powerfully influenced the course of criticism, especially through his book *Experience and Poetry* (1906). Dilthey's long and productive career began with the publication of his monumental *Life of Schleiermacher* (1868), in which Schleiermacher's contributions to hermeneutics were recognised and reworked in historical and fully secular terms. Many of Schleiermacher's notebooks, drafts and lectures were not published until the twentieth century, and it was through Dilthey that his work first became widely known.

Dilthey's hermeneutics offered a distinctive method for the human sciences (*Geisteswissenschaften*, the German equivalent of J. S. Mill's 'moral sciences'). He stressed the historical dimension as a way of obtaining an 'objectivity' at least analogous to that claimed by the natural sciences; but the historical dimension was bound up with his extension of the notion of *Erlebnis*, or 'lived experience', developed by Schleiermacher and the Romantic writers. *Erlebnis* was not simply 'experience', but the conscious grasp of it by a creative imagination in an aesthetic form capable of expressing its precise nature. Form necessarily belonged to the time in which it was elaborated, and for that very reason every artist had to discover the form appropriate for what he or she wished to express. This process of hermeneutic discovery had been described by Tieck as characteristic of Shakespeare. Against the old strictures that Shakespeare had misunderstood the rules of drama, such as the three unities, Tieck replied that Shakespeare had discovered the rules appropriate to his own *Erlebnis*. Every life situation, when its nature is full understood, corresponds to an art form. This became known as 'immanent form'.

Dilthey attempted the delicate task of elucidating the 'lived experience', the form which it created, and its historical occasion. Through the exploration of historical facts, events and world views the inward experience of the artist was illuminated, while the unique quality of a moment of historical time could in turn be understood only through such inward experience. The double movement from the individual to the general and from the general back to the individual is another version of the 'hermeneutic circle': knowledge of human behaviour, according to Dilthey, must always partake of this kind of reciprocity or mutual confirmation.

Dilthey's contribution to the theory and criticism of drama lies not only in his theoretical hermeneutics, but also in his analysis of modern drama and practical criticism of individual dramatists. His elucidations of genre formation are particularly interesting. He gives a hermeneutic definition of drama as the extreme case that brings 'the limits of understanding' into view. The limits are implicit in the mode of presentation. A work of art forms an inner pattern; although this is not chronologically sequential, we can grasp it only in the linear sequence of reading it or hearing it within time. As he puts it:

> If I read a play, it is as with life itself. I stride onwards, and the past loses its clarity and distinctness. So the scenes are lost in obscurity. The principle is: only in so far as I maintain the connection, do I achieve a unified overview of the scenes, but then I have only a skeleton. The perception of the whole I approach only through taking it up into my memory, so that all the connecting moments are gathered together.[1]

The process of *Verstehen* ('understanding'), then, is a continuous alternation between whole and part which can never be completed. In short, drama is of all art forms the one that comes closest to the conditions under which we must understand our own experience, which begins to escape us even as it takes place. Each moment is in danger of separation from the last.

It is clear that a play poses the hermeneutic dilemma even more starkly when seen in performance than when read, though every act of reading can only take place over time and so is subject to the same problem. Thus the written text is pressed in the direction of the oral text, the performance text, the spontaneity of the text of life itself. This is one of the most powerful effects of general hermeneutics. Not only are there texts to be read that are not written (those of history and culture), but the model for the text itself is the performance. It is particularly significant that the limiting case is taken as the model. Thus, as in other modern critical tendencies, the performance text emerges as central not only to drama, but to the interpretation of literature within and as a mode of culture and ideology. Dilthey would have diagnosed the convergence of different critical tendencies on the idea of 'performance' as revealing the characteristic world view of our own time. Hermeneutics remains committed to the elucidation of criteria and procedures for 'reading' the text as newly defined.

Dilthey was among the first to analyse the emergence of a distinctively 'modern' drama with its roots in the eighteenth century. He was the first to grasp the importance of Friedrich Hölderlin (1770–1843), formerly known only as a lyric poet. Dilthey's critical explorations of Hölderlin's work as a novelist, playwright and theorist of drama began the process of establishing Hölderlin's reputation as one of the greatest European writers of his time. Dilthey wrote of him in

Experience and Poetry as the originator of the lyric *Bildungsroman* (a novel centring on the hero's 'education' in life – a genre first defined and named by Dilthey) and still more as the pioneer of a form of tragic drama that had not been understood in his own day, but belonged to the future.

Dilthey, as we would expect from his hermeneutic definition, saw drama as crucial for modern literature in general. Racine, he argued, had originated the 'psychological drama', which Goethe, in his plays *Iphigenia* and *Tasso* (based on the inner experience of the poet), had further developed. Dilthey nevertheless felt that the new form of tragedy had come to full expression only in the work of Hölderlin. His play *Empedocles*, his writings on the form of modern tragedy in his notes on Sophocles' *Antigone* and *Oedipus*, and his translations from Sophocles present a formidable statement of the collision of the modern mind with the forms of Greek tragedy. As Dilthey roundly declared, one must abandon all those yardsticks by which Hölderlin's drama would be found undramatic; for he founded a new conception of dramatic action:

> Hölderlin's *Empedocles* carried on the inward drama of the psyche begun by Sophocles, Racine and Goethe. He goes beyond them on the way to an unfamiliar goal, which even today no one has attained. It is the history of our psyche, which is more significant than the tale of all our particular sufferings and successes. Where it comes to fulfilment in a human being, it is sovereign and lonely, and the noise of the world penetrates to it only in distant, vague tones.[2]

It was the solitary, however, who heard most clearly the voice of his own time. In Hölderlin's play, Empedocles, the Greek philosopher who committed suicide by flinging himself into the crater of Mount Etna, achieves a hermeneutic vision. He attains not a reconciliation through death, but a 'Hegelian death', the reversal of consciousness, 'the transition, through mediation, to a higher level of consciousness, which in Empedocles' case is historical consciousness'.[3]

His 'lived experience' is the leap into historical consciousness. Hölderlin's formulation of the nature of tragedy, however, preceded Hegel's conception of the clash of two irreconcilable and equally valid ethical positions, and while influencing it remained distinct; if the notion of a unity falling into division is common to many thinkers and poets of the time, for Hölderlin this takes the form of a specific encounter between the divine and the human, in which revelation of the divine takes place as a struggle in which unity is momentarily reasserted only to fall away. Such encounters take place at moments of crisis in history, and usher in a new phase of life. The cataclysm of the French Revolution had an impact on the imagination of Hölderlin and his generation that can scarcely be overemphasised.

Dilthey, however, in perceiving the value of the radical revision carried out by Hölderlin, failed to apply his understanding to Romantic drama generally. In particular, he failed to see the far-reaching effects of the revaluation of Shakespeare on the practice of Romantic dramatists. Surprisingly, he thus ignores perhaps the most wide-ranging and pregnant example of hermeneutic interpretation in literary criticism. He sets Shakespeare as a man of the Renaissance in opposition to Hölderlin and his contemporaries, rather than seeing the continuity of their views, and in particular the correspondence between *Hamlet* and his own recognition of the interiority of drama.

The new Shakespeare and the beginnings of modern drama

The critical revaluation of Shakespeare which made him the great representative 'modern' writer, the equal if not the superior of the classics, the source of a new model of dramatic action and character, and the touchstone of imaginative power, was carried out in Germany by Herder, Schiller, Goethe, the Schlegels and Tieck, in England by Coleridge, Hazlitt, Lamb and De Quincey, and in France, by Hugo, de Stendhal, Vigny and de Musset. As this list demonstrates, the influence of the new conceptions of Shakespeare was widespread, and playwrights throughout the nineteenth century worked in the light of them. This has not always been recognised, for the plays that emerged were based on principles that seemed to reverse the very conception of drama: the suspension of action (elevating this characteristic of *Hamlet* into a model rather than a puzzling flaw to be explained away); the non-linear, interior quality of action, in direct opposition to Aristotle; the mingling of tragedy and comedy; the banishing of the 'unities' and the restoration of the theatre of the imagination; the conception of character as an element in a unifying world view that lent the play an 'organic' wholeness. As a result, many new plays we now think of as pillars of the modern repertory were little performed and little known until near the end of the century, or indeed until the twentieth century.

The hermeneutic notion that the artist grasps his own inner experience and creates from it the rules appropriate to it was developed by Tieck, through his experience as translator of Shakespeare. Such experience represents not the artist's passivity, but his activity, for in understanding his experience he finds a form for it, and so expresses his independence of existing convention. In so doing, of course, he expresses his historical context: he is the authentic voice of historical change. As Tieck put it, 'Every life situation, if its true nature is grasped, is an art form. Only when embodied in a form can it be grasped, even by its creator.' His model for this process was Shakespeare. We see here the intimate connection between the emergence of hermeneutic understanding and the freeing of Shakespeare from the critical canons of the neo-classical school of drama.[4]

The drama of the psyche became the dominant form when the belief in an immortal soul with a capacity for an independent afterlife broke down; the decisive argument was formulated by Kant in the *Critique of Pure Reason* (1780). Hermeneutics as the art of salvaging the impermanent, temporal and fragile became the art of asserting the coherence of the transient mind. As the temporal quality of succession supplies the definition of drama in Dilthey, so time supplies the theme and structures of Tieck's plays, and leads to his characteristic forms of irony. His irony, fragmentation and self-criticism are the source of what have become known in Brecht's terminology as 'alienation effects'. These effects do not merely serve to 'break the illusion', but betoken the condition of a self always threatened with loss of its own presence, significance and continuity, and faced with the constant need to reconstruct what has become alienated. For Tieck, as his extensive Shakespeare criticism shows, this quality was exemplified by Shakespeare's characters, in particular the rapid shifting of tone from tragic to comic and back, and the pervasive presence of the marvellous, dream and fantasy. For Tieck the playwright, Schleiermacher's hermeneutic analysis of the crisis of the self was rooted in Shakespearian dramatic practice.

Georg Lukács: the hermeneutics of modern drama

Dilthey had only sketched in the outline of the modern 'drama of the psyche'. His lead was followed by Georg Lukács, the leading twentieth-century sociologist of literature, in his first published work, *The Evolution of Modern Drama* (1908).[5] Lukács, a Hungarian, is best known in the English-speaking world for his work on the novel, but in his complete range of criticism drama comes a close second in the number and range of his references to it, and stands first in theoretical significance.

His book was the first full account of the nature and development of modern drama, and it is charged with the excitement of the theatre at that crucial moment. Lukács was one of the founders of the Thàlia Theatre in Budapest; in 1905 he worked as an assistant director and dramaturg, and translated Ibsen's *The Wild Duck* into Hungarian. Modelled in part after Antoine's Théâtre Libre in Paris, the Thàlia shared the objective of presenting the work of the new dramatists: Ibsen, Strindberg and Gorky. But the Thàlia was also a theatre for the people, playing at union halls until the authorities stopped it on the grounds that the enterprise presented a fire hazard.

The 'new drama', according to Lukács, is historicist, bourgeois and individualistic, in strong contrast to the drama of community animated by religious feeling that had dominated previous eras. The historicist interest emerged in the history plays of the *Sturm und Drang* movement, especially Goethe's *Götz von Berlichingen* (1773). Its bourgeois sympathies became evident in Lessing's *Emilia Galotti* and later Schiller's *Cabal and Love*, with their opposition to the rule of the aristocracy; and its individualism, apparent in the way that the years intermingle and even change places, is exemplified by Lenz's *Soldiers* and *The Schoolmaster*, where the conflict of generations usually associated with comedy, sharpens into a tragic and irreconcilable clash of world views. Presiding over this change were the French *philosophes*, especially Diderot, whose plays, dialogues and theory of acting forwarded his opposition to the *ancien régime*, and their German counterparts, especially Herder, Goethe's mentor in his student days. In the criticism of the time, these shifts were already associated with Shakespeare's original genius.

Lukács, however, like Dilthey, failed to perceive that the leading edge of the new theatre was the reinterpretation of Shakespeare. He continued to view the Greeks and Shakespeare as 'objective', and to contrast both to the subjective, reflective tendency of later European literature; this attitude, stemming from one phase of Schiller's criticism, was confirmed and underscored by Lukács' later immersion in Hegel and then Marx.

Yet the analysis of each of Shakespeare's plays as a 'world' in itself was taken over by Lukács and generalised through the Diltheyan hermeneutic analysis of dramatic time:

For the stage has turned into the point of intersection for pairs of worlds distinct in time; the realm of drama is one where past and future, no longer and not yet, come together in a single moment. What we usually call the present in drama is the occasion of self-appraisal; from the past is born the future, which struggles free of the old and of all that stands in opposition. The ends of each tragedy sees the collapse of an entire world.[6]

Thus temporal discontinuity and multiple perspective can sharpen into a new tragic form.

At the same time, the stress on the historical brought about a shift towards tragicomedy, for in the daily course of events the genres are not separated. Again the Shakespearean example provided a model. Schiller's *Wallenstein* (1799) is a masterpiece of this period and shows how Schiller's admiration for *Julius Caesar* and for *Hamlet* produced a historical hero who fails to act at the crucial moment and so determines the course of European history. Hegel's notion of the hero as a world-historical character who necessarily falls victim to the historical process is foreshadowed by *Wallenstein* and exemplified by Grabbe's *Napoleon* in the 1820s. The events of the revolutionary period enforced a powerful sense of the failure of conventional notions of heroism. Büchner's *Danton's Death* is a study in the psychology of the new 'hero'.

The increasingly unheroic nature of the protagonist is closely linked with the disabling of the springs of action and the enfranchisement of the drama of the psyche. Where tragedy was previously brought on by the particular external direction taken by the will, in the new drama the mere act of willing suffices to induce it. Modern drama is a drama of the will itself. As the formation and continuity of the self became problematic, 'the bare fact of being able to will at all was a manifestation of personality and brought about the clash with the surrounding order of things that had previously required external action'.[7] Thus 'the bare fact of Being begins to turn tragic'. The later Lukács interpreted this in political terms; but for the non-Marxist world Samuel Beckett has come to exemplify this aspect of modern drama.

Each evolutionary phase of mankind culminates in a clash of world views that constitutes tragedy, according to Lukács. But modern drama also explores new possibilities of form. Schleiermacher and Schlegel, in proposing the link between self-knowledge, poetic form and the world, are not asserting the link as straightforwardly given but stressing the divisions within contemporary life that the active imagination of alien experience had to overcome. For Lukács, it was Goethe who fully grasped this for the drama in the problematic form of *Faust*, which invents its own form, 'the Drama of the Human Species', akin to the French 'epic of Humanity' and pointing towards Ibsen's *Peer Gynt* and Shaw's *Back to Methuselah*. For Lukács, as his *Faust Studies* show, it was precisely the Hegelian perspective of a philosophy of history depicting the dynamic succession of 'forms of consciousness' that prescribed the dominance of the dramatic in modern literature.

Thus Dilthey's hermeneutic principle 'the human being knows himself only in history, never through introspection'[8] is worked out in detail by Lukács' analysis of the history of modern drama. For him, that history passed through Hebbel to Ibsen. All knowledge is historicised but as an ever-changing ungraspable present. As external and internal aspects of character become less firmly related, the fragmentation and disorder of character is exacerbated. As Lukács shrewdly remarks of the 'intimate theatre' or chamber play (most familiar to us from Strindberg, whose model for the disproportion between public and private was Shakespeare's *Julius Caesar*), it displays a profound contradiction: 'As drama becomes increasingly an affair of the spirit, it increasingly misses the vital centre of personality.' This leads to a further radical displacement in the development of the action: 'Since the vital centre of character and the intersecting point of man and his destiny do not necessarily coincide, supplemental theory is brought in to contrive a dramatic linkage of the two.'[9] This problematic becomes a major theme of modern drama.

Domestic and private drama thus has the capacity to reflect the clash of world views as effectively as great historical dramas. Strindberg aimed to show this in his historical cycles as well as in his chamber plays; Ibsen does it in (to take one example) *Rosmersholm*, Chekhov in *The Cherry Orchard*, Musil in his brilliant and too little known play *The Visionaries*. Yet in no case could the whole character find a sufficient outlet and expression in action. His very destiny was a curtailment of his psychic drama.

Into the present: the heirs of Dilthey

Lukács was the founder of one of the two major branches of twentieth-century hermeneutics, the branch which runs through the cultural

critics of the Frankfurt School to Jürgen Habermas, its greatest current exponent. The founder of the other was Martin Heidegger, an
existentialist philosopher. In his epoch-making book *Being and Time*
(1928) he provided an analysis of the human condition, the state of
Being-in-the-world, that contributed powerfully to the understanding
of existential extremities and exerted a far-reaching influence on
modern literature. Heidegger, although he did much to extend the
notion of the hermeneutic circle, was more concerned with elaborat-
ing a new 'ontology' than with methods of explication. He took up
Dilthey's interest in Hölderlin and interpreted Hölderlin's translations from the Greek dramatists in terms of his own views; apart from
this, however, he did not write directly on drama.

More immediately important for drama were his followers, especially the philosopher, critic, playwright and novelist Jean-Paul Sartre.
From the 1930s until his death, Sartre strove to bring together the two
branches of hermeneutics: Heidegger's existential analyses and the
left-wing critiques of ideology. His play *Huis Clos* (*No Exit*), for
example, in the manner of the intimate theatre of Strindberg, analyses
secular Being in its ultimate state, a hell of its own making; *Les
Mouches* (*The Flies*) adapts the story of Orestes for wartime France.
His most extended critical work on modern drama is his existential
psychoanalytic study of the playwright and novelist Jean Genet. In
his *Critique of Dialectical Reason* (a convenient translation of a
section of which is available as *The Question of Method*) he gave an
account of his hermeneutic method, which is applied on a monumental scale in his study of Flaubert, *The Idiot of the Family*, in which he
seeks to place the writer's own world vision within the enabling (and
disabling) frameworks of his time.

Lukács survived to play a powerful part in the debate after the
Second World War, when the two branches of hermeneutics, both
deriving from Dilthey, battled over the future. The 'human sciences'
themselves seemed compromised by the use made of them by the
Hitler regime. A fresh start was sought through the reinterpretation of
Dilthey. Important new contributions were made by Hans-Georg
Gadamer in *Truth and Method* (1960). Gadamer's reinterpretation of
Aristotle's mimesis in terms of a conception of hermeneutic under-
standing that has its basis in *Spiel* ('play', including dance and
gesture) is directly relevant to the theatre.

The battle raged not only over theory but also over interpretation of
Hölderlin's poetry and plays. A concerted effort was made to rescue
Hölderlin from the suspect role of representative of the *German*

spirit. The brilliant and intricate analyses of Heidegger's interpretations of Hölderlin by the leading surviving member of the Frankfurt School, Theodor Adorno, and by Peter Szondi forced a revision of the standard edition of his works. Hölderlin came out of his isolation once and for all, as his sympathy with the French Revolution was documented. This hermeneutic battle royal needs to be told at greater length. For the drama, it resulted in the recognition at last that Hölderlin's plays were eminently stageworthy. Brecht's production of his *Antigone*, a play seen as a political protest by the individual against the state, was a landmark; and in 1979 the annual Berlin theatre festival featured no fewer than three productions of the same play. The 'text' of Hölderlin had been wholly reconstructed for a new time.

The present

At the present time, the two leading theorists of hermeneutics are Paul Ricoeur and Jürgen Habermas. Ricoeur, trained in France, has brought the more recent social sciences, especially psychoanalysis, to bear on the hermeneutic reading of both texts and action, or human behaviour in general. He has been particularly interested in the hermeneutics of demystification or decoding of a meaning presented to the interpreter in the form of a disguise. The modern 'masters of suspicion', Marx, Nietzsche and Freud, look upon the contents of consciousness as in some sense 'false' and on its symbolic expression as a dissimulation; their methods of hermeneutic analysis are aimed at uncovering the (often unpalatable) truth. The 'human sciences' are disciples of interpretation, not scientific explanation. The true 'self' may be revealed through the enactment of desire, the resurgence of archaic fantasies, the clearing of 'false consciousness' and the exploration of utopian possibilities. Ricoeur's theory of metaphor enables him to mediate between the 'decoding' of consciousness and the restoration of its symbolic expressions. This is clearly of great value both for the interpretation of plot and character in drama (for example, Ibsen's and O'Neill's explorations of the 'life lie'), and for theatre games and acting-methods.

Habermas belongs to the branch of hermeneutics associated with the critique of social practice and cultural expression. In *Knowledge and Human Interest* he shifted the centre of hermeneutic interest from Dilthey's psychologism to the investigation of the language of communication. In this he joined with the mainstream of Anglo-American philosophy. How does language embody the modes of social and cultural control of the 'world vision' of the public? How does it reflect the production of 'false consciousness' or 'bad faith' by groups defending their own status and interests? In his *Theory of Communicative Action* (1981) he explores the history of the notion of 'rationality' in West European society, and more specifically its use in the social sciences. The urgent question he poses is whether the techniques of social control, including the manipulation of the meaning of language by the media, make a mockery of the notion of 'rationality'. Can art, and in particular a public art such as the theatre, survive to play a critical role? Can the theatre speak the language of authentic communication?

The concern for modes of communication generally, including ritual, gesture, mime and play, has borne fruit for theatre practice. The hermeneutic interest in ritual is long-standing, stemming from a recognition of the way in which the Christian community had created and maintained the significance of the biblical text and the authority of the Church through ritual enactments. When the meaning of the text and the authority of the Church were eroded by historicism, the question of how to 'read' ritual action became even more pressing. The relation of ritual to Greek and other forms of tragedy, not least the medieval drama, which for a long time was viewed as having arisen from the dramatic opportunities afforded by the liturgy itself, became a major concern of drama criticism. So did the question of whether a modern tragedy could be evolved from history, rather than from myth and its ritual enactment. Ritual has gradually lost its necessary connection with religion and has been secularised in various ways which are vital to the theatre.

The first phase of the transition from religious terms to anthropological and secular ones was accomplished by Ludwig Feuerbach in *The Essence of Christianity* (1841). His stress on the rituals of everyday life (eating, washing, etc.) as pervaded by the sacral had a powerful impact on literary practice, as well as on the development of the social sciences. Ritual in primitive and evolved societies became a major concern of anthropology, in theory and in the field. Nineteenth-century interpretations of Hölderlin stressed the quality of ritual in his plays and poetry and saw him as preparing the way for Wagner. Early in the twentieth century the Cambridge School of Anthropology played an important role in stressing the ritual origins of drama; its influence on T. S. Eliot is well known.

In recent times, this model for drama has been much criticised and attempts have been made to formulate more secular definitions of ritual. Some of the most exciting works of recent social history have been conducted in terms of secular ritual and the Russian critic Mikhail Bakhtin's notion of 'the carnivalesque' as an element in social life. One of the most important points Bakhtin makes is that social ritual may be critical of society, and even in some instances lead to revolution; it is not always merely a confirmation of the *status quo*. This insight has been applied to specific historical instances – for example, in Emmanuel Le Roi Ladurie's widely read books *Montaillou* and *The Carnival at Romans*.

The most influential of recent anthropologists, Victor Turner, has worked extensively on the relation between ritual and drama. Turner pays explicit allegiance to Dilthey. Social anthropology owes much to Dilthey in any case; but Turner returned to Dilthey for the foundation of an 'anthropology of experience' in which anthropological and literary insights and practice are combined. As Turner puts it:

> The anthropology of performance is an essential part of the anthropology of experience. In a sense, every type of cultural performance, including ritual, ceremony, carnival, theatre, and poetry, is explanation and explication of life itself, as Dilthey often argued. Through the performance process itself, what is normally sealed up, inaccessible to everyday observation and reasoning, in the depth of sociocultural life, is drawn forth. A performance, then, is the proper finale of an experience.[10]

The importance of Turner's analysis in terms of Dilthey's 'five moments of experience' lies in his choice of 'social drama' in his primary category, through which both ritual and theatrical drama are interpreted. Although some recent literary critics have made Turner the starting-point of theories of drama opposed to the tradition of ritual origins, Turner's own writing, in *The Ritual Process* and *From Ritual to Drama*, points rather to the broadening and secular historicisation of 'ritual': the social drama is the experiential matrix from which the many types of cultural performance are generated. Thus he can continue to hold that drama originates in ritual, though it is no longer specifically religious ritual.

'Social drama' is described with reference to a wide range of examples, but especially instances drawn from his field experience in Africa. Turner sees social dramas as containing a recognisable sequence of moments: first, a regular, norm-governed social life is interrupted by a *breach* of rule; this leads to a state of *crisis* which splits the community into contending factions; third, *redress* is sought, through juridical ritual, or military processes known to the society; this may bring about, finally, *reconciliation*, or *consensual recognition of irremediable breach.*[11]

Turner further attempts to distinguish between social drama and theatrical drama, on the basis of much recent writing on the nature of play and the emergence of the notion of 'leisure' in modern societies. The contrast drawn between 'work' and 'play' in modern society does not, it is argued, arise in fully ritualised societies, where both play and work are incorporated into recognised ritual cycles and rhythms; in such societies 'play' is far less a matter of choice. In modern society, theatre is only one of an array of choices, in which ball games are at least as good as poetry. Turner suggests that in completely ritualised societies the elements of disorder and chaos are given rein in Saturnalian or Lupercalian revelry, charivari or institutionalised orgy, but are contained by such means, whereas in modern post-industralised societies 'leisure' activities may be not merely inverted images of society but actually subversive.

In what sense this is so needs exploring; the Frankfurt School has made a more searching and pessimistic analysis of the probability of ideological 'bad faith' in a commercialised culture with its mechanically reinforced stereotypes. It is also doubtful whether Turner's distinction between social drama in ritual and social drama in theatre is adequate. But it is clear that the hermeneutic moment has contributed to this conception of the active role of theatre in modern society. In this earlier work Turner stressed the moment of free '*communitas*' within ritual initiation ceremonies of the 'rite of passage' kind as the experience fundamental to both ritual and theatre.[12] In both ritualised and modern societies, he insists, the individual plays a vital role as the representative and perpetuator of the culture, after a perhaps painful and prolonged effort to understand it.

Turner has some very suggestive notions for theatre; even if we stop short of the 'ethnographic' theatre he recommends, his 'hermeneutic Catherine wheel' of anthropological theatre is an enticing image.[13] The closest that theatre has come to it, outside Turner's own theatrical experiments in the United States, is Peter Brook's *The Ik*, an attempt to dramatise the anthropological work of Colin Turnbull in *The Mountain People* (1972). The Ik are an African tribe that invented new, harsh social modes to cope with their gradual extinction through starvation. The use of Dilthey's 'five moments' for the reconstruction of alien experience to explore the implications of social drama suggests a still-unexplored range of games, exercises, rituals, ceremonies and spectacles. Many of the current theatre games and exercises used for the training of actors – as described, for example, in Clive Barker's influential *Theatre Games* – could with profit be reorganised in this light.

Indeed, one practical aspect of theatre to which hermeneutics has made a great, if largely unrecognised, contribution capable of much further development is that of acting-technique. The method of acting that has developed in conjunction with the demands of modern drama is best known in the formulations of Stanislavski. But its history reaches back into the eighteenth century, to Diderot's theories of the kind of acting appropriate for bourgeois drama, and their adoption around 1808 by Mikhail Schepkin, an actor who afterwards collaborated with Gogol. Gogol's own 'Advice to Those who Would Play *The Government Inspector* as it Ought to be Played' (1846) sums up pungently the new demand for naturalness, abandonment of rhetoric and exaggerated gesture, and an imaginative inwardness, even for comedy and satire. The actor must read the play over until he has a sense of its unity; the characters must be understood from within to be genuinely comic. 'Root out caricature entirely and lead them to understand that an actor must not *present* but *transmit*.' This distinction is vital. 'He must, first of all, transmit ideas, forgetting about a person's oddities and peculiarities.' The pregnant notion of reconstruction of the self of another is strikingly put: 'No one is comic to himself.' The actor must strive to 'capture those aspects that are common to all mankind'. He ought to consider the purpose of his role, the major and predominant concern of each character, what it is that consumes his life and constitutes the perpetual object of his thoughts, his *idée fixe*. So, 'one should first grasp the soul of a part not its dress'.[14]

This idea was clearly well suited to the presentation of the new problematic heroes, tragicomedy and ironic modes, as well as Gogol's grotesque satire. It was also in full accord with the concern of the new drama to reflect the circumstances of ordinary life, even where the consequence was genuine tragedy.

The name commonly given to this kind of acting was 'realism'. But this is misleading, even if its opposition to naturalism is fully grasped. Especially in it more developed form, sometimes known as 'psychological realism', as worked out by Stanislavski from 1906 to 1932, it shows the characteristics of general hermeneutics: a new inwardness of experience and its uniquely appropriate expressive form, combined with a scientific grounding in the functions of brain and nervous system, affective psychology, theories of the will, language and speech, rhythm and movement. After even a brief sketch of the development of modern hermeneutics, Stanislavski's famous 'processes' have a very familiar ring.

1.   The 'actor's reading' prepares his 'will' to play the role by rousing his enthusiasm.
2.   His 'searching' casts round for psychological material, in his own experience and that of others, for the re-creation of the role.
3.   In the process of 'experiencing', the actor creates invisibly, for himself. He 'must adapt himself to this alien life and feel it as if it were his own'.
4.   In 'physicalising', the actor creates visibly, for himself.
5.   In 'synthesising', the actor puts together his inward experiencing and his external physicalising of it, for others.

This process is described in detail in *Creating a Role*.[15]

The hermeneutics of 'actor's reading', as well as Stanislavski's explorations of the sub-text as projection of the psyche, needs to be taken into account by current hermeneutics and reader-response theory. While the act of reading has received a great deal of attention, recent criticism has concentrated on the reader of fiction. To be sure, the powerful creative activity attributed to the reader of fiction has often assimilated him to the creative activity of the writer; yet the powerful re-creative force of the 'actor's reading' has received little attention, despite concern with the 'phenomenological reader', the 'super-reader', the 'implied reader', and so on. Consideration of the 'actor's reading' would also be a vital step towards an understanding of the 'audience's reading' of the fully realised performance text.

Recent work on sensory communication and non-verbal hermeneutics needs to be drawn into descriptions of processes 4 and 5, for Stanislavski's scientific sources are now much in need of revision.

Stanislavski's own development of his system through successive 'lived experience' of failure in particular productions or roles shows the artist in the process of discovering his authentic form. 'The

Production' offers an excellent example of an organic event, one that can be seen and analysed as a whole. Stanislavski's transforming experiences are of special importance because the productions in which he underwent them were of plays which now form part of the core repertory of modern drama: Chekhov's *The Seagull*, Shakespeare's *Julius Caesar* (in which he played Brutus), Turgenev's *A Month in the Country*, and Knut Hamsun's *Drama of Life*. His personal struggle helped to shape the strikingly international canon of the modern theatre.

It is clear that the new canon is made up not only of new plays, but also, even primarily, of 'hermeneutic appropriations' – that is, plays translated from other times and places, familiar texts more or less radically adapted, and, perhaps most of all, adaptations using fresh 'performance texts'. Hermeneutics and its recent critical offshoot, the aesthetics of reception, offer the most satisfactory theoretical framework for understanding this essential aspect of modern theatre. In adaptation one may read off more accurately than anywhere else what the working playwrights and theatre practitioners of the day see as demanded by and appropriate to the contemporary audience. This is particularly true of Shakespeare adaptations, which by themselves suffice to sketch a hermeneutic history of the stage – from Tate's seventeenth-century *Lear* and Garrick's eighteenth-century performance texts, to Brecht's *Coriolanus*, Ionesco's *Macbeth*, Charles Marowitz's provocative rewritings for the Open Space Theatre, Edward Bond's *Lear*, and Botho Strauss's unnerving revision of *A Midsummer Night's Dream* as *The Park*, which opened in Berlin in 1984. Some of the leading playwrights of the century (for example, Brecht) have devoted a considerable proportion of their work to it; Tom Stoppard's *Rosencrantz and Guildenstern Are Dead* is an example of an adaptation of Shakespeare that succeeds in being a play in its own right – indeed, the author's best play to date. Stoppard has described his feeling that he is a 'writer' only in so far as he has published one novel; to prove his point, he cites the case of his television film 'Squaring the Circle', a different version of which he sold to American television only to find the director of the original entering an irate claim for authorship.[16]

It is a commonplace to say we have a director's theatre; it would be truer to say we have an adaptor's theatre, in which directors play a significant role as adaptors of performance texts. Active direction is a subject of adaptation. Consideration of these matters in the context of hermeneutics could lead to a new branch of theatre studies. If hermeneutics has been thought to have a special care for finding and preserving the text in its entirety, as earlier it provided the justification for using the uncut Shakespeare text, it has an equal care for the adaptation, especially in the extreme forms favoured by the present *avant-garde*.

Recent hermeneutic theory has suggested that 'application' (as opposed to 'understanding' and 'critical explication') in literary hermeneutics is represented by translation. It could well be argued that practical application is in fact adaptation, of which translation is one aspect, the process of adaptation often concealed behind protestations of fidelity to the original. Current translation theory stresses the transforming aspect of translation, or 'radical translation', where a writer draws from a foreign writer or tradition the nucleus for a wholly independent work;[17] and even the most faithful rendition is a different work when placed in new historical circumstances. One could go further to propose that application is performance itself, in which the process of adaptation encounters the contemporary audience through whose response we create the 'text for our time'.

In conclusion, it is clear that from the start hermeneutics has been a dynamic method closely related to praxis, intensely responsive to historical change and concerned with communicative processes, including non-verbal as well as verbal gesture and regarding translation and adaptation as nodal points at which the nature of the interpretative community can be 'read'. It is the theoretical framework most precisely suited to the needs of the theatre, for it has developed in response to the same set of conditions as modern theatre itself.

NOTES

1. Wilhelm Dilthey, 'Plan der Fortsetzung zum Aufbau der geschichtlichen Welt in den Geisteswissenschaften', 4: 'Hermeneutik', *Gesammelte Werke*, VII, pp. 225–7.
2. Wilhelm Dilthey, *Experience and Poetry*, p. 415.
3. Paul de Man, 'Heidegger's Exegeses of Hölderlin', *Blindness and Insight* (London, 1983) pp. 264–5.
4. Ludwig Tieck, *Buch über Shakespeare*, pp. 293–372.
5. This book has been translated into German, but only parts of it have been published in English. A brief selection translated from a revised version published in German in 1914 can be found in Eric Bentley (ed.), *The Theory of the Modern Stage* (Harmondsworth, Middx, 1968; rev. edn 1976) pp. 423–50; and one complete chapter, translated by Stanley Mitchell, appears in E. S. Shaffer (ed.), *Comparative Criticism*, VIII (Cambridge, 1986).

6. G. Lukács, 'The Sociology of Modern Drama', in Bentley (ed.), *The Theory of the Modern Stage*, pp. 426–7.
7. Ibid., p. 430.
8. Dilthey, *Gesammelte Werke*, VII, p. 279.
9. G. Lukács, in Bentley (ed.), *The Theory of Modern Stage*, p. 436.
10. Victor Turner, *From Ritual to Theatre: The Human Seriousness of Play* (New York, 1982) p. 13. Dilthey's 'five moments' are described on pp. 13–15.
11. Ibid., p. 92.
12. See especially Victor Turner, 'Liminality and *Communitas*', *The Ritual Process* (London, 1969). The source of the term '*communitas*' is the existential philosopher Martin Buber's *I and Thou*, p. 193.
13. Turner, *From Ritual to Theatre*, p. 98.
14. *The Theatre of Nikolay Gogol*, pp. 169–70.
15. See S. Moore, *The Stanislavsky System: The Professional Training of an Actor* (Harmondsworth, Middx, 1976).
16. Tom Stoppard, 'Real Books, Real Authors: A Letter to the Editor', *The Author* (Summer 1984) pp. 61–2.
17. Reuben Brower, 'Translation as Parody', *Mirror on Mirror: Translation, Imitation, Parody* (Cambridge, Mass., 1974).

FURTHER READING

Introductions to hermeneutics of literature

Eagleton, Terry, 'Phenomenology, Hermeneutics, Reception Theory', *Literary Theory: An Introduction* (Oxford, 1983) pp. 54–90.
Hirsch, E. D., Jr, *Validity in Interpretation* (New Haven, Conn., 1967).
Hoy, David Couzens, *The Critical Circle: Literature and History in Contemporary Hermeneutics* (Berkeley, Calif., 1978).
Palmer, Richard, *Hermeneutics: Interpretation Theory in Schleiermacher, Dilthey, Heidegger,* and *Gadamer* (Evanston, Ill., 1969).

Hermeneutic Critics

Dilthey, Wilhelm, 'The Development of Hermeneutics', *Selected Writings* (Cambridge, 1976) pp. 246–63.
Gadamer, Hans-Georg, *Truth and Method*, ed. Garret Barden and Gohr Cummings (New York, 1975).
Heidegger, Martin, 'The Age of the World View', trs. Marjorie Grene, in *Boundary*, 4, no. 2 (1976).
Ricoeur, Paul, 'What is a Text? Explanation and Understanding' and in 'The Model of the Text: Meaningful Action Considered as a Text', *Hermeneutics and the Human Sciences,* trs. and ed. John B. Thompson (Cambridge, 1981) pp. 145–64, 197–221.

Schleiermacher, Friedrich, 'On Translation', in *German Romantic Criticism* (Oxford, 1982) pp. 1–25.

Hermeneutics of Drama

Lukács, Georg, 'Historical Novel and Historical Drama', *The Historical Novel*, trs. Hannah and Stanley Mitchell (Harmondsworth, Middx, 1969).

Palmer, Richard, 'Towards a Postmodern Hermeneutics of Performance', in Michel Benamou and Charles Caramello (eds), *Performance in Postmodern Culture* (Madison, Wis., 1977).

Peck, Jeffrey M. (compiler), 'Bibliography of Hermeneutics: Literary and Biblical Interpretation', in E. S. Shaffer (ed.), *Comparative Criticism*, v (Cambridge, 1983).

Plessnor, Helmuth, *Laughing and Crying: A Study of the Limits of Human Behavior* (Evanston, Ill., 1970).

Turner, Victor, *Dramas, Fields and Metaphors* (Ithaca, NY, 1974).

——, *From Ritual to Theatre* (New York, 1982).

——, 'Universals of Performance' (1982), in E. S. Shaffer (ed.), *Comparative Criticism*, viii (Cambridge, 1986).

Chapter 7

The Concept of Dialogue

MAGNUS FLORIN, BO GÖRANZON and PER SÄLLSTRÖM
Translated by Kevin McCafferty

In 1985 the Royal Dramatic Theatre (Dramaten) and the Working Life Centre (Arbetslivscentrum), both in Stockholm, began a series of seminars on the question of dialogue. That two such different institutions – the one devoted to producing theatre, the other to the analysis of the role and impact of technology on working life – should co-operate in this way may seem surprising, yet it is not really that strange. Theatre has always used technology for its own purposes, and, as a former Director of the Royal Dramatic Theatre, Erland Josefson, has pointed out, theatre has a 2000-year-old tradition of passing on knowledge and experience through dialogue.[1]

Four themes have been central to the seminars:

— the world of dialogue;
— the inner dialogue;
— dialogue and enlightenment;
— unfinished dialogue.

This chapter examines some of the insights which have emerged in discussion.

The world of dialogue

Raphael's fresco *The School of Athens*, housed in the Vatican, portrays numerous groups of people, young and old, either engaged in lively conversation or listening intently to it. There is an awesome gulf between this scene and that presented by the modern person in solitary 'dialogue' with his/her personal computer. One is prompted to ask, what will be the consequence for our essentially human ability to develop and communicate thought, insights and knowledge through the medium of dialogue if there is, in practice, increasingly little dialogue between people? Will the theatre find itself becoming the guardian of the culture's capacity for dialogue?

Dialogue as a means of clarifying issues within a community of human beings, and as a basic component of their reality, has been the subject of pictorial, dramatic and literary works since antiquity, the most famous example perhaps being Plato's record of the Socratic dialogues. An attempt, however, to elaborate on the phenomenon of dialogue itself as a basic component of human life and reality, as something essential to human existence, an attempt to generate a philosophy of dialogue, belongs mainly to the twentieth century. It concerns the deadlock between subjectivity and objectivity which was in evidence by the beginning of the century, and the tension between unity and fragmentation of knowledge.[2]

The word 'dialogue' is used more loosely in everyday speech than in philosophy. It has become the fashion to describe any kind of communicative interaction – between people, between men and machines, or between interconnected systems in general – as 'dialogue'. But this may be to overlook an important distinction, one to which, historically, philosophy has often drawn attention – the distinction between simple communication (or 'information transfer') and authentic dialogue. Not all conversations between two people are necessarily dialogues in the sense of a meaningful exchange of ideas. A conversation may consist of 'empty' words.

The medium of transformation

Dialogue is the medium of transformation in the theatre. Dialogue occurs where roles meet; it sets them in motion, leading to unexpected shifts. As it proceeds in a necessarily dialectical way – a to and fro – words, thoughts, events and characters change form and even meaning. Consider how skilfully Iago uses his dialogue with Othello to transform everything he hears and sees. Through dialogue, the theatrical space becomes a place where firm positions and sharp contours cannot be maintained. King Duncan thinks Macbeth's castle 'sweet' and 'pleasant', not knowing that death awaits him within its walls.

Such examples demonstrates an essential aspect of the concept of dialogue: its innate capacity to record and explore differences. In dialogue, differences of perception and of ideology can appear and be played off against one another, both within individuals and between people; it sets all their various voices and contradictions in motion. However, out of contradictory dialogue consensus can emerge if three preconditions are met: *understanding, community* and *honesty.* We achieve a dialogue with each other if we are to reach a positive agreement based on a shared and honest understanding of terms. Nothing reinforces a sense of community more than dialogue based on such preconditions.

Seen this way, dialogue is perhaps the opposite to ideology, or certainly to ideology of a doctrinaire kind. Unlike ideology, dialogue does not require the total articulation and explication of a belief system. There is something unnervingly disciplinarian about creating an ideology; it involves an element of coercion, an insistence on adherence to the letter of a creed. Just as theatre by its very nature explores the plurality of truth, so dialogue admits of differing points of view. In the dialogue seminars discussed in this chapter we were interested in defences against demands for clear articulation. There is always a dark side of life which defies precise description. People cannot be adequately described using the rules of formal logic alone.

The growing technological base to our culture in both work and education often takes a reductionistic, rational view of language, knowledge and experience. In terms of philosophy and cognitive theory, it can be said to rest on a simplified model, in which man is represented as a Cartesian atom in a large but accurately mapped universe. When we speak of the concept of dialogue, it is to question that model. We focus instead on reciprocity, the mutual dependence from which we emerge and in which we live. This mutual dependence emphasises that what we are is the product both of ourselves in an intrinsic sense but also of I–you or I–other relationships. An actor is only an actor in the presence of an audience.

The inner dialogue

In one of Plato's earliest dialogues, *Euthyphro*,[3] Socrates tries to understand and characterise devotion. Euthyphro, a religious prophet, gives examples from his work. In this dialogue, Socrates pushes Euthyphro to formulate the rules defining an act of devotion, Euthyphro claims to be able to judge what an act of devotion is, but cannot articulate or explain the rules his judgement obeys. In Plato's views, experts (in this case a religious prophet) have consciously acquired rules of analysis of their field of expertise, but in the case of time have forgotten them. The philosopher's task is to rediscover the principles that determined their actions by observing what they do.

It is generally argued that Plato and Socrates undervalued practical work in favour of the abstract intellect. This argument rests on the case, developed notably in *The Republic*,[4] that people with practical skills cannot explain in words how they perform their tasks. The carpenter making a chair is unable to explain how he goes about it, but the philosopher is able to discuss the conceptual idea of the chair and its use: the philosopher is more articulate than the carpenter and is therefore his superior. The relatively recent rise of the theatre director rests, in a sense, on a similar presumption: that actors are not good at describing what they do and therefore require some figure to help them express themselves.

Expression is not, however, merely a matter of deploying words for factual purposes: it also involves rhetoric, and on the question of rhetoric even Socrates has some doubts. In *Gorgias*,[5] he casts suspicion on the art of rhetoric, arguing that it is not an art at all; rather it is a practical skill, the driving-force of which is the speaker's desire for recognition and acceptance by the listener. Given this, it is surprising that he does not reassess his attitude to skill in a more positive light. Challenged on this point, Socrates denies that he takes a negative view of practical skills: he merely points to the indisputable fact that practical skills can be used in the service of evil as well as good. What he ignores is the craftsman's capacity for intuitive, or inarticulable, insight into what he is doing and why. In the craftsman's mind and actions a deep connection is established between his skill as such and its moral and cultural value. Yet he can be aware what purpose his activity is supposed to serve without necessarily translating such an awareness into words. It is this internal dimension, the *inner dialogue*, that characterises his true skill. It is only when we are prepared to accord inner dialogue its place in our analysis of the dialogic process as a whole that we can achieve a deeper understanding of what it involves.

There are two issues here. On the one hand, there is the relationship between language and action, the extent to which we can describe our actions in words. On the other hand, there is the demand for inner dialogue, for insight and reflection, not least of a moral kind. How do these two levels relate to one another? Where do they contradict, or interact with, each other? The philosopher Ludwig Wittgenstein resolves these questions in his theory of knowledge as follows: 'Perhaps what is inexpressible (what I find mysterious and am not able to express) is the background against which whatever I could express has its meaning.'[6] His understanding of the issue owes much to his reading of Shakespeare.

Shakespeare

In his lecture 'Shakespeare's Dialogue'[7] Leif Zern looked at Shakespeare's use of dialogue as a dialectical system for analysing the world. Shakespeare appears to stress the need to challenge cultural pressure to conform to strict and immutable rules. This is not to say that he advocates anarchy, but rather that he shows that through dialogue rules may constantly be questioned and, where appropriate, redefined. Order and disorder are two sides of the same system; together they serve renewal and fertility in a society threatened by death and sterility. Shakespeare is aware of the mechanisms that widen the gulf between language and people's experience. He makes no simple oppositions between conflicting classes or interests. Crises occur when concepts become confused, when cracks appear in the very system of norms and agreements that make man capable of uniting around a communal understanding of reality.

Shakespeare describes the crisis that occurs when agreement ceases, when language and reality no longer coincide. What is essential is not what is, but what may or will be. The truth is never to be found at the point of departure. It grows in motion. It springs from meetings and passage – in ties that are constantly being undone and incorporated in new contexts. This motion cannot be frozen and translated into a formula.

Rousseau

In her lecture 'Rousseau's Theory of Knowledge'[8] Eva-Lena Dahl analysed the view of knowledge developed by Jean-Jacques Rousseau, discussing, in particular, the two levels, the linguistic and the moral, mentioned in connection with Plato's dialogues. In her interpretation, Rousseau's arguments indicate that he sees thought as a process in which man experiences reality as actual and moral at one and the same time. According to Rousseau, description and evaluation of reality are intimately related to the process of thinking itself. In such a context, the parameters of dialogue may be set by the dialectic of description and evaluation, of imitation and analysis. Such a dialectic is fundamental to theatre.

Rousseau says that if we divide knowledge into two kinds, *acquired* and *common*, common knowledge is infinitely greater than acquired knowledge. We have a shared, perhaps preconscious, knowledge the scope and depth of which tends to be underestimated, even ignored, by the educated. Theoretical knowledge is enriched by experience, but without it it creates chaos. For Rousseau, the question then arises of whether the acquired concepts of scientific theory are adequate to describe reality, or whether our descriptive language may not be better traced back to a base of common knowledge that our senses can experience. The distinction is analogous to that between telling and showing in theatre, the balance of opinion lying with the belief that theatre should show, not tell.

Diderot: dialogue and enlightenment

Denis Diderot, one of the leading figures of the Age of Enlightenment in France, was one of the principal influences on the establishment of the Stockholm dialogue seminars because of his perception of the relationship between theatrical (or aesthetic) skill and technological skill. He expresses one aspect of this relationship in his dialogue *Rameau's Nephew*:[9] 'He who needs rules will never get far.'[10] It is not prescriptive rules of behaviour that advance understanding, but experience, just as books on how to act have little bearing on how in rehearsal an actor actually experiences the development of his role. It is constant practice that develops and deepens expertise. Reflection becomes imperative: 'That cannot be. There are some days when I am forced to reflect. It is a sickness that must be allowed to run its course.'[11]

Rameau's Nephew is a dialogue on the conditions necessary for creativity. It is also an inner dialogue between Diderot himself and his two personae, the Philosopher, who represents logical, calculable common sense, and Rameau, the vulgar bohemian on the bottom rung of society, who nevertheless has an affinity with the deeper layers of sensitivity in his personality. Diderot examines what maintains the links between these two different characters. Rameau attacks the Philosopher for retreating from complex reality into abstract personal isolation. The Philosopher criticises Rameau for his excitement at pantomime pranks, and his inability to exercise any practical skill. The conflict is not resolved. The final position is that the discord is irreconcilable.

The mastery of *Rameau's Nephew* resides in the fact that Diderot does not take sides in the struggle between the senses and the intellect, but rather uses this struggle to represent the complexity and contradiction which exist at various levels in each individual. Each of us may find our creative rhythm by maintaining the balance between the two which is suited to our own temperaments and abilities.

Dialogue and disagreement

True dialogue requires a certain measure of scepticism: disagreement as a principle is not simply reconcilable with dialogue – it is one of its preconditions. Dialogue involves opening oneself to criticism of one's own assumptions, a refusal of bigotry; it also involves a sensitivity to the communication process as a whole, and in particular to how opinion or knowledge is received by the listener or the learner. There is an ever-present temptation to retreat into the dream world of monologue. Retreat into abstractions offers an escape from unpleasant reality, a kind of fantasy retreat from dialogue to monologue. Such a retreat can only damage the self and the culture on which the self depends.

The reception process can take place over time, sometimes with distorting effects. When Allan Janik uses Offenbach as an example to illustrate how the price of isolation is self-deception and dehumanisation, it may seem bizarre, not to say absurd, because we tend to link Offenbach's work with the sickly sentimentality and general inertia of the world of operetta.[12] Yet a distorted reception process, reflected in ill-conceived performance traditions, must bear a large part of the blame for our inability to see the pertinence of Offenbach's satire. This satire is embedded in the very nature of his music, which operates on a dialogic principle of debate between his respect for and parody of existing musical values.

Dialogue in music, as in other art forms, exists partly as a debate between traditional and modern values, partly as a dialectic between the physical and the aesthetic nature of sound itself. Music as an acoustic phenomenon is balanced by the musician's appreciation of music as an essentially autonomous phenomenon, which emerges on a higher level of structural complexity than that described by the physicist. The essence of music can only be grasped by listening to it.

Our feeling for music is, according to the musicologist and philosopher Victor Zuckerkandl, very close to our sense of time: 'There is hardly anything that can tell us more about time and temporality than can music. . . . Music is temporal art in the special sense that in it time reveals itself to direct experience.'[13] Thus 'the truth of music, like that of mathematics, consists in this, that it serves us as a key to understanding the world we live in'.[14] So a dialogue between music and science is, in this very profound sense, fruitful and meaningful.

An element of dialogue in music itself can be found in the relation between the tune and words of a song: 'Words that are sung are not empty. Something that remains silent in word merely spoken begins to flow, to vibrate; the words open and the singer opens to them. It is as though the tones infuse the word with a force that reveals a new layer of meaning in them that breathes life into them . . . .'[15] Words express confrontation, whereas melody expresses togetherness. In the song, things that are separated meet: person and thing – the speaker and the spoken word – come into direct contact. The melody added to the word does not cancel out the word, but makes it penetrate to a greater depth, separateness becomes togetherness.

Zuckerkandl argues that: 'The dimension disclosed by the tones can certainly be called "inner life", but this is not the inner life of the subject as opposed to the object; it is not the inner world of the self but of the world, the inner life of things.'[16] This is why the singer experiences inner life as something he shares with the world, not as something that sets him apart from it. Music prevents the world from being entirely transformed into language, from becoming nothing but object, and prevents man from being nothing but subject. The performance process as a whole may be held to exemplify similar principles.

Dialogue and the knowledge of familiarity

Only those who reflect on their experiences develop the ability to deal with new situations similar to those they have already experienced. This is what the rehearsal process is about. An unreflecting, purely habitual action does not transcend what has once been learned. Knowledge requires inner reflection, a dialogue with things. Martin Buber gets to the crux of the matter when he claims that, in order to know, for example, what 'pain' is, we must ourselves actually have it, and become distanced from it at the same time. Just such a paradox is described by Diderot as fundamental to acting: at one and the same time the actor is, and is not, the role he plays. This may point to a necessary paradox in the acquisition of all knowledge.

This paradoxical process of learning is not confined to the arts. Natural science, too, requires an element of dialogue. Or rather two elements: it is both research and a dialogue between researchers. The dialogue validates the objectivity of the observation, making it something that is not the creation of one individual, but, rather the result of what occurs 'between' what they each experience. As Goethe observed, the advancement of science is more the advancement of society, culture, time. It is a dialogue between researcher and research object, the object being nature, which 'thus speaks . . . to herself and to us through thousands of phenomena'.[17] The picture of nature as speaker, as 'respondent' to the researcher's questions, may be felt to be playful anthropomorphosis, but is not without foundation, for the crucial element of all experimental research is reference to what exists outside the research itself – to other authorities, to things outside our control, even to the unpredictable. This is a dialogue. Nature's 'answer' is something I receive in answer to my research, my questions.

This may be the principle that separates experimental from purely speculative research. No physicist in his heart and soul imagines that we should be able to sit down and 'think out' reality. There are things that can only be understood through 'looking at how things behave'. It is an element of pure factuality, accessible not in abstract thought alone, but only through observation, through touch, contact, making connections.

Dialogue and language: the unfinished dialogue

Can we say that the concept of dialogue, as refined in the Stockholm dialogue seminars, is now ready for the Great Synthesis? On the contrary: the seminars merely established some of the variety of elements that constitute dialogue. Above all, disagreement and conflict are what gives the concept of dialogue its vitality. If we are prepared only to adopt that part of conversation which reinforces our preconceived opinions, 'that in which we recognise ourselves', we are holding a monologue with ourselves, not a dialogue with others. The growth of knowledge, in all its various shades and forms, is a process that requires an inner life of its own, its own breathing-rate. It can never be a uniform, linear progression. It cannot be built of prefabricated building-blocks, one on top of the another. Nor can it be fed with series of data like an electronic calculator. Dialogue is the concept that expresses the dynamics of knowledge. The purpose of dialogue is to set knowledge in motion, to stop it fossilising into empty forms.

Against this background, what are we to make of the relationship of dialogue to language? There is a contradiction in linking the concept of dialogue so self-evidently to conversation when dialogue in its very essence is wordless, belongs to the silence beyond all words. In order to solve this paradox, we require a deeper understanding of what language is and of man's relations to language, which is where theatre may come to the rescue.

NOTES

1. Erland Josefson, 'Theatre and Knowledge', given as the opening speech of the conference 'Culture, Language and Artificial Intelligence', June 1988, published in Bo Göranzon and Magnus Florin (eds), *Culture, Language and Artificial Intelligence* (London, 1989).
2. The question of a philosophy of dialogue has been touched on by most of the famous philosophers of our time – for example, Husserl, Heidegger, Gadamer, Sartre, Jaspers, Marcel – and was at the very core of the philosophies of Martin Buber, Ferdinand Ebner and Ludwig Wittgenstein.
3. Plato, *Euthyphro*, trs. Harold North Fowler, intro. by W. R. M. Lamb (London, 1914).
4. Plato, *The Republic*, trs. with an introduction by H. D. P. Lee (Harmondsworth, Middx, 1955).
5. Plato, *Gorgias*, trs. W. R. M. Lamb (London, 1925).
6. Ludwig Wittgenstein, *Culture and Value*, 2nd edn, ed. G. H. von Wright in collaboration with Heikki Nyman, trs. W. Peter Winch (Oxford, 1980) p. 16e.
7. Leif Zern, 'Dialogen hos Shakespear' ('Dialogue in Shakespeare'), lecture delivered at Dramaten, 28 October 1985.
8. Eva-Lena Dahl, 'Synen pa Kunskap i Jean-Jacques Rousseaus

Ideologie' ('The View of Knowledge in Jean-Jacques Rousseau's Ideology'), lecture delivered at Dramaten, 11 November 1985.

9. Denis Diderot, *Le Neveu de Rameau* (Rameau's Nephew), chronology and preface by Antoine Adam (Paris, 1967). This work was written intermittently between 1761 and 1764 and eventually published, after Diderot's death, by Goethe.

10. Diderot, *Le Neveu de Rameau*, p. 105.

11. Ibid., p. 134.

12. Allan Janik, 'Offenbach: Konsten mellan Monolog och Dialog' ('Offenbach: Art between Monologue and Dialogue'), lecture delivered at Dramaten, 12 May 1986. The lecture was based on two books by Victor Zuckerkandl, *Sound and Symbol* (Princeton, NJ, 1956) and *Man the Musician* (Princeton, NJ, 1973).

13. Zuckerkandl, *Sound and Symbol*, p. 200.

14. Zuckerkandl, *Man the Musician*, p. 352.

15. Ibid., p. 40.

16. Ibid., p. 56.

17. J. W. von Goethe, Preface to *Die Farbenlehre* (1810), quoted from *Goethe's Theory of Colours* (Cambridge, Mass.).

Chapter 8

Theatricality and Technology: Pygmalion and the Myth of the Intelligent Machine

JULIAN HILTON

Can machines think? No, said Descartes. Why not? Machines can give the appearance of thought in that they can be made to imitate man, but there is a fundamental difference between this power of imitation and real thought. This difference is best illustrated by analysing the relative speech capacities of men and machines. Men can speak; even the most stupid of us can communicate vastly more effectively than other life forms. This power of speech is the outward manifestation of reason; and reason is what makes man. So, Descartes concludes, 'we ought not to confound speech with the natural move-ments which indicate the passions and can be imitated by machines as well as manifested by animals'.[1] Descartes's position is open to a number of serious challenges, not least in the way that it misinterprets the intelligence level of many animal communication systems. But in one respect his test is unassailably right: a machine must be capable of acts of reasoning and speech independent of the programmer before it can be deemed intelligent. All else falls under his criterion of imitation.

This test is hard-line and controversial; in her book *Artificial Intelligence and Natural Man*, despite an avowed purpose in seeking to counteract 'the dehumanising influence of natural science'[2] Margaret Boden later tacitly admits that little of what she writes about would pass the Cartesian test: 'Computer simulations in general attempt theoretical modeling of psychological function and structure, rather than ontological mimicry of mental reality, and it is in these terms alone that they should be assessed.'[3] But even Professor Boden is bolder than many who count themselves specialists in Artificial Intelligence (AI), for whom AI is merely an extension of automated engineering.[4]

There is a hitherto neglected area of inquiry for AI research which may bring us closer to an answer. This is the area of simulation of behaviour, or, more precisely, the area of theatre. Theatre is, to borrow Boden's phrase, 'ontological mimicry of mental reality'. Aristotle, one of the first great systematic scientists, devoted a great deal of thought to attempting to codify what he regarded as the highest achievement of human intelligence, tragic poetry. Man's urge to create such poetry grew naturally, so he argued, from his urge to imitate, children's play (which so often involves role-play) leading to theatrical plays. 'Imitation is natural to man from childhood, one of his advantages over the lower animals being this, that he is the most imitative creature in the world, and learns by imitation.'[5] (This propensity to imitate suggests that the imitative function Boden currently assigns AI may be the early part of a learning-curve which will lead AI in due course to satisfying Descartes's standards.) Tragedy functions, according to Aristotle, as a complex system for simulating emotions, the purpose of which is to effect a catharsis in the audience, who leave the theatre cleansed.[6] For this to happen, the actors must persuade their audience that, even though they are acting, the emotions they generate are real. So theatre rests from the outset on the paradox that it is simulated and yet real. When an actor plays Oedipus, he clearly is not the real Oedipus – if ever there was one. Yet, unless he convinces his audience that he feels as Oedipus felt, his performance is accounted a failure.

At the point at which an actor so identifies with his role that he collapses his own self into that of another, he has stopped acting and become simply mad. Theatre always depends on the maintenance of a critical distance between the actor and his role. Yet this distance must never be allowed to break the contract of probability between the actor and his audience – the contract that rests on the belief that theatre only functions if the actor can persuade the audience, and the audience signal to the actor, that they both believe that the events of which they are part could probably have happened, or happen.

This special nature of theatre has fascinated many scientists, including Bacon, Descartes and Diderot, so the suggestion which I now make that AI (as a science) needs to investigate theatre needs no particular defence. The possibility exists that the special nature of theatrical intelligence, which underpins the cultural success of theatre in society, will offer clues to the satisfactory replication of human reasoning and creativity in machines, or, alternatively, help demonstrate that such a possibility is unrealisable. It may also be that theatre offers us, by analogy, an intermediate test of intelligence, somewhere between Descartes's hard-line position, and the imitative position taken by Boden and many others.

There is another aspect to theatre which qualifies it for our attention: theatre is as much about technology as about art, the technology enabling the art. As such, it offers an integrated and integrative model of human intelligence of a kind fundamentally useful to AI.

The theatre machine

While theatre is an art form, it is an art form intrinsically enabled by technology. Viewed another way, theatre is a complex aesthetic machine, dedicated to the representation of the imaginable through performance. The performer and all the apparatus of staging – set, lighting, costumes, effects – are components of this machine, driven by the collective imagination. Since the industrial revolution, perhaps even since the beginnings of the new science in the seventeenth century, machines have, however, been associated in men's minds with dehumanisation, with dark Satanic mills, with the decline of human values. So theatre has rarely faced its own technological nature despite the fact that its mass appeal has rested as much on its technological as on its aesthetic genius, because it has wished to range itself on the side of civilised values in conflict with the world of enterprise and machines.

Theatre's affinity with science is great: both science and theatre can be broken down into pure and applied skills, the Jesuits, for example, justifying the centrality of theatre in their curriculum for this very reason; rehearsal pursues a similar strategy to scientific research, proceeding by observation and empirical testing to the adoption of 'least worst' hypotheses. Yet, for reasons it is not my purpose here to unravel, since the seventeenth century science and theatre have drifted further and further apart.

The challenge of AI may change this. In effect, AI is the attempt to replicate in machines the reasoning and imaginative powers of the human brain, which presupposes that we have some knowledge of what these powers are. In fact, science knows very little in this respect, while theatre, admittedly more tacitly than explicitly, has been exploring the problem of representing or simulating one person's behaviour by means of another for thousands of years. AI may learn a great deal from examining the theatre's extended investigation into the nature of human intelligence.

For Shakespeare and his contemporaries the metaphoric proposition that the world is a stage (*theatrum mundi*) hardly needed defending. It was clear that all human action was played out on a great universal stage, and that men and women were actors in some great play. The Globe Theatre was the globe in microcosm; it was a cipher for representing all knowledge. Since the seventeenth century, theatre has lost confidence in its own centrality as mediating metaphor of reality as it has dissipated its energies in a fruitless debate about the relative significance of words and images. It has also lost its power as a universal metaphor, embodying all knowledge in a single proposition: 'All the world's a stage'.

The way the microcosmic Globe Theatre functioned was as a great space-time machine, driven by the energy of the imagination:

> Can this cock-pit hold
> The vasty fields of France? Or may we cram
> Within this wooden O the very casques
> That did affright the air at Agincourt?
> O pardon: since a crooked figure may
> Attest in little place a million,
> So let us, ciphers to this great account,
> On your imaginary forces work.
> (*Henry V*, Prologue, 11–18)[7]

Not only can the space-time machine cram northern France into the cockpit, it can also journey us around England and France in the course of a few lines. It does this through the agency of the fancy:

> Play with your fancies; and in them behold
> Upon the hempen tackle ship-boys climbing;
> Hear the shrill whistle which doth order give
> ...... still be kind
> And eke out our performance with your mind.
> (*Henry V*, III, Chorus, 7–9, 34–5)

This summary by Shakespeare of how theatre works – technology mediated by the visual and oral imagination of the audience – helps pinpoint the role of the imagination in any representation of human intelligence, for without it the boards of the Globe can never represent the great world stage. This single observation has profound implications for any attempt to create an intelligent machine, for, however much knowledge is stored within the machine, it will be our imagination which determines our sense of its intelligence.

The nature of the theatrical imagination is itself central to the equation of the world with the stage, for it rests, as Diderot recognised, on a central paradox, that the actor both is and is not the role he plays. It is essential to the naturalistic effect of theatre that the actor represent his role with sufficient plausibility for the audience to believe in it. Yet it is equally essential that a distance be maintained between actor and role, so that the act of representation can simultaneously be one of analysis. I suggest that a similar paradox, perhaps even the same one, lies at the heart of the problem of machine intelligence. A machine intelligence is simultaneously a naturalistic representation of human intelligence and a representation of its meta-principles, principles that no single intelligence can possess in entirety. (An expert system, for example, must feel like a single expert while embodying the knowledge of many experts.) As a result AI is qualitatively different from human intelligence and may, therefore, be hard to define in terms intelligible to human intelligence (perhaps it will take an intelligent machine to recognise another intelligent machine).

The resolution of Diderot's paradox lies in the principle Keats identified as the core of Shakespeare's art, 'negative capability',[8] the capacity of a work of art to support many, even conflicting, meanings. There are as many ways of playing Julius Caesar as there are actors to play the role, and yet the role is always the same role. As Schiller expresses it, this very relationship between the specificity of the individual actor and the generic nature of his role is the basis of the aesthetic concept of 'play' which he advances in his 'letters' *On the Aesthetic Education of Man*.[9] It is through the specific that the generic is created and legitimated.[10] These two positions identify for us further tests of the efficacy of the replication of human intelligence in machines. First, the artificial intelligence must be capable of supporting conflicting interpretations of the same data; secondly, the specificity of its 'mind' must be one criterion of its generic validity.

In the context of the Shakespearian view of the theatre as a space-time machine it is hardly surprising that one theme in theories of performance is that of the actor as intelligent machine. Practitioners in the theatre, such as Heinrich von Kleist, have advanced the theory that there is a fundamental and beneficial relationship between acting and animated puppetry, while the founders of modern scientific method, Bacon and Descartes, have expressed deep interest in the practice and metaphor of theatre. One of the purposes of the intelligent machine is to imitate actual human behaviour; another is to explore potential human behaviour. When we sit in Shakespeare's Globe, we are being asked to imagine what it would be like to travel in time and space, questions which, in a sense, create the aesthetic and imaginative preconditions for the technological realisation of such travel.

We are also being asked to imagine something else, the possibility that it may be man, not God, who is the author as well as measurer of all things. Such a claim was not original: Marlowe's *Dr Faustus* was about this issue. 'Here, Faustus, try thy brains to gain a deity', says Faustus to himself in his opening speech.[11] The claim concerns theatre every bit as much as it concerns science. The playwright is a kind of god in that he writes words for imaginary people which then cause real people (actors) to bring those words and those people to life. In this sense he goes beyond actual into potential human experience. Technological research is also informed with this sense of the pursuit of the imaginable. If we can imagine flying to the moon, how can we actually do it? If we can imagine creating intelligent machines, how can we actually make them? One myth which addresses itself to these problems is that of Pygmalion and Galatea, the statue that comes to life. Under the influence of Freud and the psychoanalysts, it has been the Oedipal myth that has dominated much of our thinking this century. Now perhaps we are moving into the age of Pygmalion.

Pygmalion and the perfect machine

The myth of the intelligent machine perhaps enters culture in the story of Pygmalion and his statue. On the one hand, the story of a statue that comes to life seems to suggest that a technologist of genius can transcend the limitations of matter, turning stone to flesh; on the other, it expresses a basic truth about all art, that an artefact, once complete, achieves a life of its own. The terms of the myth are simple. Pygmalion, a sculptor of genius, is dissatisfied with all the women he encounters so sets out to make his own. He carves a woman in the image of Aphrodite and then begs the goddess to breathe life into his stone. She accedes and Galatea comes to life.

The affinities of this myth with the theatre are fundamental. A writer writes a script in which certain characters are created, in a sense in ideal form. Then, through the agency of actors, these characters come to life, in the process developing beyond what the original creator conceived for them.

The story is, like any good myth, much harder to interpret than to narrate. In terms of a Platonic theory of mimesis the statue is profoundly ambiguous. Within Plato's aesthetic, a statue, like any work of art, is an imitation of an imitation of an ideal original. Since each imitative step is a degradation from the ideal, Pygmalion's statue cannot but be essentially flawed. Yet this statue must be a special case, because it is not an imitation of a real woman but rather represents Pygmalion's ideal woman, the woman who has all the qualities real women lack, Aphrodite. The statue is beautiful because it imitates a divine ideal. The ambiguity is not, however, confined to the question of beauty and ideal form. Pygmalion presumably is seeking for a woman of ideal character (content). What he creates is a woman of ideal form. His assumption that beauty is a guarantee of sweetness of temper is surely profoundly flawed, as indeed some versions of the myth indicate by making Galatea turn quickly into a typical woman, a shrew. Here the myth becomes something quite different. Pygmalion is a mysogynist at best, a hard-line chauvinist at worst. His attitude to all women is reflected in his refusal of any of them, and his eventual disaffection with Galatea is not her fault at all, but his. In such terms, Pygmalion is the ultimate hate object of all feminists.

From the perspective of AI research, the myth challenges us to think of the knowledge-representation process in triangular terms – of expert, representational medium and expertise. Pygmalion, the expert, wishes to capture in stone, the medium of representation, the ideal woman, his expertise or idealised knowledge. His purpose is initially merely to record in stone this knowledge, but, as his success in representation grows, so do his ambitions. Finally, he brings his knowledge base to life, only to discover that it was as flawed as any other. What is more, it is not his own hand, but that of a goddess, which effects the transformation from statue to woman. We are, in effect, in the same position as Shakespeare leaves us, that there has to be an agent of transformation to turn any mere representation into an active and independent creation. That agent is the imagination.

In *The Advancement of Learning*, Bacon, a committed Platonist, leaves us in no doubt that any positive interpretation of Pygmalion's ambition is inimical to Platonic notions of truth:

> Here therefore, is the first distemper of learning, when men study words and not matter. . . . It seems to me that Pygmalion's frenzy is a good emblem or portraiture of this vanity: for words are but the images of matter; and except they have life of reason and invention, to fall in love with them is all one as to fall in love with a picture.[12]

Pygmalion's frenzy is, however, crucial to the AI debate, for the risk of all AI research is that of mistaking the forms of intelligence for intelligence itself. Is the mere pursuit of AI a 'frenzy', or can the danger Bacon points out be avoided? The answer may not perhaps be sought in science, but may lie in aesthetics. Bacon's objection to Pygmalion's behaviour is that he lavishes his affection on a representation with no original, a signifier with no signified. This is contrary to reason, or so argues Bacon. This may be so, but falling in love with pictures is a habit not confined to the stage or to fiction. Quite the opposite, it seems a basic tenet of powerful myths that they share with the Pygmalion story the property of being representations of actions and people who have no original, as Hamlet, Don Juan and Dr Faustus have no real-life models. In effect, therefore, the successful creation of the ideal woman from stone undermines the mimetic theory of art. If they undermine mimetic aesthetics, do they also undermine mimetic theories of intelligence? For, if they do, the representation of human intelligence in machines may require aesthetic as much as or even more than scientific skills.

Pygmalion, knowledge transfer and de-skilling

One influential aesthetic version of the Pygmalion myth is George Bernard Shaw's perhaps most popular play, *Pygmalion*, made even more popular by the musical *My Fair Lady*, which locates the myth within a feminist and a socialist context of great significance to the progress of AI.[13] It concerns a (natural) language expert, Professor Higgins; his colleague, Colonel Pickering; and an object of experiment, Eliza Doolittle. Higgins bets Pickering that with his expert knowledge of language he can transform Eliza from Cockney to duchess in six months (rapid knowledge transfer). He succeeds, to the extent that all London society is inflamed with Eliza's success.

The levels of the transformation are complex, engaging with Eliza's appearance, her manners, her speech and her thoughts. First, Eliza is made to look like a duchess, in which respect the original terms of the Pygmalion myth are observed. The ideal woman has to look beautiful. But Shaw's observation informed him that, especially in English society, class is determined less by appearance than by accent and linguistic practice, and Eliza's success is therefore significantly more dependent on her voice than her face. So, secondly and thirdly, Eliza is made to move and sound like a duchess. Yet at this point the wisdom of Bacon's warning against 'frenzy' becomes apposite. Higgins may have made Eliza sound like a duchess, but what she actually says (her thoughts) remain unchanged: she still thinks and swears like a Cockney, but in perfect aristocratic tones. This is the danger of studying words divorced from meaning.

We may characterise this flaw in Higgins' knowledge-transfer system as the flaw of virtual knowledge. Higgins assumes that if he teaches Eliza to speak like him she will also think like him. His system apparently functions perfectly until it is required to display real intelligence, a problem unforeseen by the programmer. At this point 'system Eliza' crashes: she is ruffled, but has not been programmed to respond to being ruffled in a polite way; so she swears. Her learning is quite distinct from her understanding. In an expert such as Higgins, the knowledge that polite diction must equal polite semantics is obvious but tacit. In the expert system Eliza, no such tactic knowledge base is embedded. Eliza's failure is not linguistic but hermeneutic and sociological. At one level, Shaw has confirmed the old adage that it is not clothes that make the person but the inner mind – or tacit knowledge. Eliza betrays herself because her tacit knowledge system is totally different from that of Higgins. At another level, Shaw seems to be suggesting that any adequate practical definition of intelligence itself is not merely specific to a given culture, but specific even to small sub-sets of that culture. Cockney intelligence is not West End intelligence; male intelligence is not female intelligence.

This exacerbates still further the problem of knowledge transfer, for it highlights the need for careful evaluation of what we might call the knowledge environment (all those factors conditioning tacit knowledge) in our study of knowledge transfer. It also returns us to another warning about knowledge transfer that Bacon issues to *The Advancement of Learning*:

> For as knowledges are now delivered, there is a kind of contract of error between the deliverer and the receiver. For he that delivereth knowledge, desireth to deliver it in such form as may best be believed, and not as may best be examined; and he that receiveth knowledge, desireth rather present satisfaction, than expectant inquiry; and so rather not to doubt, than not to err; glory making the author not to lay open his weakness, and sloth making the disciple not to know his strength.[14]

This 'contract of error' indicates that, in Bacon's view at least, knowledge transfer is synonymous with error.

Higgins commits a system error of a second kind, equally relevant to AI, which is intrinsic to his own specialised memory system. He has perfected a use of sound-recording onto discs which constitutes his linguistic knowledge base. He teaches Eliza from this knowledge base. The problem, however, is that the crucial part of the knowledge base was configured many years earlier and is now out of date. Eliza learns a static, and therefore archaic, English: when she goes to take her place in society, linguistically it can already detect the difference between Queen Victoria's English and its own. Higgins' expert system crashes for a different reason, because it relies on a static knowledge base. Expertise is by implication always dynamic, a fact which contradicts any claim that an expert system will be able to solve a given task once and for all.

The third phase in Eliza's transformation comes when Eliza begins to discern what has happened, that she is capable of playing a duchess but is in fact no such thing. She first intuits this problem when she realises that her new linguistic expertise has in fact de-skilled her in a different respect: 'I sold flowers. I didn't sell myself. Now you've made a lady of me I'm not fit to sell anything else. I wish you'd left me where you found me.'[15] Will this be the fate of all users of expert systems, that they de-skill themselves? Eliza's response to this frightening possibility is to contemplate suicide. She runs away from Higgins, though, fortunately, straight in to the arms of a nice young man, Freddie. This action leads to two challenges Shaw delivers back to his Pygmalion, Professor Higgins. The first is that, despite the apparent success he has achieved in raising Eliza socially to such a level that she can marry Freddie as an equal, the economic reality is that she will support him in their married life, not *vice versa*. On one level, this is a perfect feminist riposte. On another, it is an indication of perhaps the most complex problem of all issues in knowledge transfer, that the recipient of knowledge, whether human or mechanical, may not do with the knowledge what the knowledge engineer envisaged. As Shaw puts it, 'Galatea never does quite like Pygmalion: his relation to her is too godlike to be agreeable.'[16] In fact, Eliza goes back to her original trade, as a flower-seller, and resists the deskilling implications of her new expertise. It is now common knowledge that one of the problems expert systems face is that they tend to be rejected by experts. Is this merely Luddite behaviour, or is it perhaps that Shaw is right – that the premise of an expert system is a godlike degree of knowledge, a feature which humans quite naturally find disagreeable?

Kleist and the theatrical perspective

The theatrical myth of the intelligent machine centres on the marionette and the marionette-like actor. The playwright Heinrich von Kleist explores this myth in a celebrated essay, 'On the Marionette Theatre' ('Über das Marionettentheater'),[17] in which he argues that the combination of human operator and mechanical actant leads to a quality of dance unattainable by the human dancer. Kleist's theory focuses on the interaction (dialogue) of the puppeteer with the puppet. This interaction he describes as a 'line' ('Linie') along which the '*soul of the dancer*' ('*Seele des Tänzers*')[18] moves. The geometric metaphor of the line is reinforced by an arithmetical analogy: 'Instead, the movements of his fingers behave in a rather artificial way compared to the movements of the puppets that are attached to them, a bit like numbers in relation to their logarithms.'[19] The analogy with logarithms points to an underlying proposition in the essay that there is a meta-language of dramatic expression which functions to specific performances as logarithms function to real numbers. This relationship in turn establishes the preconditions for the dialogue between puppet and puppeteer through which communication with the audience takes place. Communication with an audience is, therefore, a function of communication between puppet and puppeteer.

The next step in Kleist's logic is to claim that through the meta-language of expression the mechanical representation of the dancer's soul can in fact transcend the limitations of any individual dancer: 'he dares claim that if a craftsman were to make a marionette according to the specification he would give him, that he could stage a dance with it that neither he nor any other skilful dancer of his age . . . could be in any position to match'.[20] The claim is analogous to Pygmalion's, that the statue he makes will be a woman superior to any the normal processes of nature can conceive. The claim is similar to that made for expert systems, that the elicitation of expert knowledge and its representation in mechanical form will in fact create a degree of expertise superior to that achievable by any human equivalent. Strikingly, what has emerged in expert systems as perhaps the central problem, discerning what it is experts actually know, is regarded here by Kleist as merely circumstantial in the representational process. This process, again distinct from current philosophies of expert system, proceeds on the assumption that the human expert will still be involved with the system once it is established.

Kleist's most problematic observation, however, lies in the suggestion that such involvement is at its most powerful and convincing when it is least conscious. The advantage the puppet has over the human is that, because it has no individual consciousness, it never indulges in 'decoration', the addition to the aesthetic ideal of a personal, and superfluous, signature of individual style. 'For decoration appears, as you know, when the soul (*vis motrix*) finds itself in a point other than the centre of gravity of the movement.'[21] There is both a cultural and a physical aspect to this argument. In a cultural sense, Kleist is attacking one of the props of Romanticism, the belief that intelligence and creativity are in some sense the product of a single, inspired mind rather than of a culture as a whole or a group within a culture. The attack is of great significance, for in our own time we are still caught in a definition of creativity and intelligence that attributes the successful generation of new ideas and concepts to single thinkers. Kleist's implicit plea is for a recognition that what and how we think are a function of our behaviour, which is itself a social and cultural construct. In such terms, the way we approach machine intelligence could be radically affected, since it would permit a definition of machine intelligence to be contextual: a machine is intelligent if it is part of the creative environment of a creative group. If we were, as individual researchers, prepared to abandon the notion of ideas as personal property, we would in consequence enhance the possibility of generating intelligent machines.

In a physical sense, Kleist rightly observes, beauty and effectiveness in performance are functions of the overall physical state of the performer as reflected in his or her sense of balance, or centredness. This in turn leads to an equation of the physical state of centredness with the psychological or spiritual sense of being 'centred', meaning a total concentration on the act of performance. Kleist sees such an equation, however, not as Schiller would, as a forward movement through the dialectic of form and content towards the imaginative free play of a transcendent, rule-free aesthetic, but rather as a falling-back into that state of grace from which we fell:

> 'Should we,' I said, a little distraught, 'therefore eat again from the tree of knowledge, in order to fall back into a state of grace?'
> 'Just so,' he replied: 'that is the last chapter of the history of the world.'[22]

The consciousness to which we must 'fall back' is one based on utter simplicity and economy of effort. This has profound implications for any definition of expertise, for it suggests that expertise at its most powerful is deeply embedded and unconscious, rather than declared and conscious knowledge. In practice, the mere process of knowledge elicitation from human intelligence, on which machine intelligence is of necessity based, violates this principle by attempting to make explicit that which cannot be articulated. The result is an inevitable degradation from human to machine intelligence, a degradation we experience in practice every time we use 'intelligent' machinery. What this may imply is that robots are good at what they do purely because they are not intelligent enough to get bored or tired. If they were, they might malfunction.

Büchner: testing the intelligence of the mechanical human

Not the least of the many innovative insights of Georg Büchner, whose short creative life set the agenda for modern European theatre, was into the nature of machine intelligence. At the close of his comedy *Leonce and Lena* the nature of human identity is bound up with the identity and psychology of machines. Valerio, the valet and Pygmalion, brings in two androids. His speech is of such significance as to merit full examination:

But in fact I wanted to announce to this high and honoured company that this very moment the two world-famous automatons have arrived and that I myself am the third and perhaps most remarkable of both, if only I really knew who I was, at which, by the way, you should not wonder, since I do not in the least know what I am saying, nor do I even know that I do not know, so that it is highly improbable that anyone is *making* me speak and that there is nothing more saying this than barrels and pipes. (*In a rattling voice*) You see here, ladies and gentlemen, two people of both sexes, a boy and a girl, a man and a woman. Nothing but art and technology, nothing but cardboard and clockwork. Each has a fine, fine spring of ruby, under the nail of the toe on the right foot; you press lightly and the mechanisms run for a full fifty years. These people are so perfectly constructed that you could not tell them apart from other mortals, if you did not know they were cardboard; one could in fact make them members of human society.

(*Leonce and Lena*, iii.iii)[23]

At one level, the speech is a comic rewriting of Hamlet's famous disquisition on the nature of man: 'What a piece of work is man'. Is man a clockwork masterpiece, or a tortured consciousness? Even were man consciousness, that proposition is so circumscribed with doubt that he can never be sure he is not in his human form merely the representation of the imagination of another form of consciousness altogether. This line, which Büchner pursues to its deliberate absurdity, is also curiosity consoling in AI terms; for perhaps our worries about defining consciousness in machines needs to be contextualised by our inability to come up with any satisfactory definition of consciousness of any kind. Do we even need to know?

At another level, the speech pursues the analysis initiated by Kleist of the relationship between acting and mechanical behaviour. There is a sense in which acting, which means speaking the lines of another, wearing the clothes of another, entering the consciousness of another, is akin to mechanical intelligence, the human body being merely a vehicle for the consciousness of another. The implication is significant: by analysing the process by which an actor assumes the consciousness of a role one may discover how a machine may be programmed to assume human intelligence. Büchner's analysis of this process of transformation of consciousness is perhaps the reverse of what one might expect a humanist to suggest: that the actor is the more human the more he faces the machine within himself. And only

by accepting the mechanical in himself can he assume the consciousness of another. For AI this might mean that we shall be able to
transfer our intelligence to a machine at the point when we accept and
understand the extent to which our own intelligence is already mechanical.

The reason why Büchner may have through this way lies in his
other area of skill, anatomy and physiology. Büchner had studied and
come to admire the sheer brilliance of mechanical man, man the
machine. And this, for all his protestations of annoyance with
Descartes, shows his debt to Cartesian thought, on which, in his brief
life, he spent a considerable amount of time and about which he
wrote at some length.[24]

Descartes and the dissociation of sensibility

In his *Discourse on Method* Descartes addresses himself to the issue
of man the machine in positive terms: 'Some persons will look upon
this body as a machine made by the hands of God, which is incom-
parably better arranged, and adequate to movements more admirable
than is any machine of human invention.'[25] In some respects, this is
just how any performer sees his own body, as a machine to be
programmed by training and rehearsal to perform tasks of great
beauty and complexity. Such a perception may offer an explanation
of the popularity of the performing arts in Western culture in that they
are widely, if intuitively, perceived to be in harmony with, rather than
in opposition to, a computer-based hi-tech culture. Until a machine
can choreograph like John Cranko or sing like Maria Callas, can it be
thought of as intelligent? The tests Descartes himself proposes are
not dissimilar:

> but if there were machines bearing the image of our bodies, and
> capable of imitating our actions as far as it is morally possible,
> there would still remain two certain tests whereby to know that
> they were not therefore really men. Of these the first is that they
> could never use words or other signs arranged in such a manner as
> is competent to us in order to declare our thoughts to others . . . as
> men of the lowest grade of intellect can do. The second is, that
> although such machines might execute many things with equal or
> perhaps greater perfection than any of us, they would, without
> doubt, fail in certain others from which it could be discovered that

they did not act from knowledge, but solely from the disposition of their organs.[26]

Yet there is a dimension to this problem which Descartes leaves unexplored, one that theatre challenges us to consider. When an actor learns a role, in a sense he (or she) has become the mechanical representation of another. He walks and talks like someone else, someone who is not himself. In a strict sense, his knowledge base of the person he represents is determined by his lines, his part. But clearly this is far from being the true extent of his knowledge.

Below the surface of his words lies the subtext of the actor's role, a potentially limitless body of tacit knowledge about what the character is like, what he would do in certain situations, even though the explicit text does not address itself to such situations or problems. When audiences witness the performance of such roles, they experience a continuous paradox, that the actor whom they are watching both is and is not the person he represents. He succeeds with his audience in as far as he convinces them that he is who he says he is. At a mechanical level, this means convincingly walking and talking like his character. But he also succeeds, as Brecht pointed out, when he does not collapse his own identity into that of his role's, but rather maintain an objectifying, defamiliarising distance.[27]

The significance of this paradox is that it offers a model of how to resolve the problem of the 'dissociation of sensibility' raised by T. S. Eliot in his reflections on post-Cartesian culture,[28] while at the same time offering a more sophisticated test than Descartes's as to the nature of machine intelligence. Eliot's theory traces back to the origins of modern science in the writings of Bacon and Descartes a fatal dissociation of sensibility in our culture, a divorce of *ratio* from *passio*, a failure to resolve the dialectic of reason and emotion in faith. This cultural divorce is effected by the principle of systematic doubt embodied in Cartesian thought.

I have suggested in this essay that we might test the intelligence of a machine according to its ability to feel human to the user, to replicate the experience of dialogue with a human mind. But this argument needs qualification in the context of my arguments about theatre. We do not expect of actors that they so utterly identify with their roles that they surrender entirely to them. We accept an undeclared simultaneity of identity and distance. The same, by analogy, may be true of machine intelligence. We may be able to accept within the spirit of our aesthetic definition of performing intelligence that a machine both is and is not like a human intelligence. In this way, the aspects of human intelligence defined as emotion and reason may not be in opposition at all, but rather be simultaneous perspectives on the same, dynamic problem. To act a role intelligently I must be able both to master the logical demands of the role and its feelings, and in rehearsal I shall pursue feelings with a developed and logical technique. The foundation of this technique, as Brecht saw it, is observation, in itself the foundation of scientific method.[29] The test of its success, as Stanislavski saw it,[30] lies in the psychological credibility with which it is communicated. These perspectives equate in a single person, the performer, the two halves of the knowledge-transfer contract examined by Bacon. The performer seeks rhetorically to persuade his audience of the verity of his performance role while at the same time using his intelligence constantly to observe and analyse whether the role stands up to his own scrutiny of it. If it does not, how can he plausibly present it to his audience?

The theory of a dissociation of sensibility in fact embodies two distinct fears for culture. On the one hand, a dehumanised and mechanical culture, premised entirely on reason and logic, threatens to fall off into the realms of Mr Spock in *Star Trek* ('too logical by half') or the excesses of Orwell's *1984*. On the other, it threatens a dissociation of a different, hermeneutic kind, that described by Bacon as a contract of error. The preoccupation with post-Cartesian mythology has been with the former problem, with such issues as whether machines can be intelligent or have souls or be compatible with humanist values. But in this essay I have examined a number of writers' attempts to explore, and perhaps explode, the myth of the intelligent machine by analysing not only the fear of the mechanical and robotic, but also the area covered by Bacon's phrase, the contract of error. On the face of it, the Pygmalion myth is about the vanity of human wishes in trying to achieve in a machine what is impossible in human beings – perfection.

But behind this problem lies another, the principle of the contract of error. It is in the very nature of Pygmalion's purpose in creating Galatea that he fail, fail not in the absolute sense of not being able to achieve anything remotely like human characteristics in his perfect machine, but in a relative sense. Pygmalion's failure is his own, and is intrinsic to the knowledge-transfer process. Galatea cannot, by definition, become what Pygmalion expects; for the act of becoming human in itself is an act of distancing from any other human identity.

Galatea's humanness is tested in the extent to which she throws off Pygmalion's intentions for her.

In a sense, the implications of this for machine intelligence are more profound than fears of a robotic culture. For it means that the real test of AI is whether or not the programme is capable of devising a strategy for refusing the commands of the operator.

NOTES

1. René Descartes, *A Discourse on Method*, trs. John Veitch (London, 1912) p. 46.
2. Margaret Boden, *Artificial Intelligence and Natural Man* (Hassocks, Sussex, 1977) p. 4.
3. Ibid., p. 55.
4. Cf. for example the emphasis of such journals as *Artificial Intelligence and Society*. On a general point of nomenclature, it may well be appropriate to count expert systems as non-intelligent in a Cartesian sense and term all such engineering-applications expert systems.
5. Aristotle, *The Poetics*, in *The Works of Aristotle Translated into English*, ed. W. D. Ross (Oxford, 1928) xi, 1448a.
6. Ibid., p. 1449b.
7. Quotations from William Shakespeare, *Henry V*, ed. Gary Taylor (Oxford, 1982).
8. Cf. *The Letters of John Keats*, ed. Maurice Buxton Forman (Oxford, 1931) i, 77.
9. Friedrich Schiller, 'Über die äesthetische Erziehung des Menschen in einer Reihe von Briefen', *Gesammelte Werke*, ed. Reinhold Netolizky v, 319–429. For Schiller there is a close interdependence of the concepts of play and machinery, the whole work being shot through with the metaphor of the state as a machine, threatening constantly to break down.
10. Ibid., p. 427.
11. Christopher Marlowe, *The Tragical History of Dr Faustus*, in *Marlowe: Plays and Poems*, ed. M. R. Ridley (London, 1955) p. 122.
12. Francis Bacon, *The Advancement of Learning and New Atlantis*, World's Classics edn (London, 1951) p. 30.
13. George Bernard Shaw, *Pygmalion: A Romance in Five Acts*, ed. Dan H. Laurence (Harmondsworth, Middx, 1986).
14. Bacon, *The Advancement of Learning*, p. 162.
15. Shaw, *Pygmalion*, p. 103.
16. Ibid., p. 148.
17. Heinrich von Kleist, 'Über das Marionettentheater', *Sämtliche Werke*, intro. by K. F. Reinking (Wiesbaden, n.d.). The original was published in four sections in the *Berliner Abendblättern*, 12–15 Dec. 1810. The translations from German are my own.

18. Kleist, *Sämtliche Werke*, p. 982. The emphasis is Kleist's.
19. 'Vielmehr verhalten sich die Bewegungen seiner Finger zur Bewegung der daran befestigten Puppen ziemlich künstlich, etwa wie Zahlen zu ihren Logarithmen' (ibid.).
20. '. . . er getraue sich zu behaupten, dass wenn ihm ein Mechanikus, nach den Forderungen, die er an ihn zu machen dächte, eine Marionette bauen wollte, er vermittelst derselben einen Tanz darstellen würde, den weder er, noch irgendeinen anderer geschickter Tänzer seiner Zeit . . . zu erreichen imstands wäre' (ibid.).
21. 'Denn Ziererei erscheint, wie Sie wissen, wenn sich die Seele (*vis motrix*) in irgendeinem andern Punkte befindet, als in dem Schwerpunkt der Bewegung' (ibid., p. 983).
22. ' "Mithin," sagte ich ein wenig zerstreut, "müssten wir wieder von dem Baum der Erkenntnis essen, um in den Stand der Unschuld zurückzufallen?" "Allerdings", antwortete er, "das ist das letzte Kapitel von der Geschichte der Welt" ' (ibid., p. 987).
23. 'Aber eigentlich wollte ich einer hohen und geehrten Gesellchaft verkündigen, dass hiermit die zwei weltberühmten Automaten angekommen sind und dass ich vielleicht der dritte und merkwürdigste von beiden bin, wenn ich eigentlich selbst recht wüsste, wer ich wäre, worüber man übrigens sich nicht wundern dürfte, da ich selbst gar nichts von dem weiss, was ich rede, ja auch nicht einmal weiss, dass ich es nicht weiss, so dass es hoechst wahrscheinlich ist, dass man mich nur so reden l ä s s t, und es eigentlich nichts als Walzen und Windschläuche sind, die das Alles sagen. *Mit schnarrendem Ton.* Sehen Sie hier meine Herren und Damen, zwei Personen beiderlei Geschlechts, ein Männchen und ein Weibchen, einen Herren und eine Dame. Nichts als Kunst und Mechanismus, nichts als Pappendeckel und Uhrfedern. Jede hat eine feine, feine Feder von Rubin unter dem Nagel der kleinen Zehe am rechten Fuss, man drückt ein klein wenig und die Mechanik läuft volle fünfzig Jahre. Diese Personen sind so vollkommen gearbeitet, dass man sie von andern Menschen gar nicht unterscheiden könnte, wenn man nicht wüsste, dass sie Pappdeckel sind; man könnte sie eigentlich zu Mitgliedern der menschlichen Gesellschaft machen.' Georg Büchner, *Sämtliche Werke und Briefe*, *historisch-kritische Ausgabe mit Kommentar*, ed. Werner R. Lehmann (Hamburg, 1972) I, 131.
24. Cf. ibid., II, pp. 137–226. Büchner's disagreement with Descartes comes down to his objection to Descartes's reliance on God as the source of reason.
25. Descartes, *Discourse on Method*, p. 44.
26. Ibid., pp. 44–5. Cf. Turing's summary of 'The Argument from Consciousness' in his paper 'Computing Machinery and Intelligence'.
27. The theme runs through Brecht's work, but see for example Bertolt Brecht, *Schriften zum Theater, 3: 1933–1947* (Frankfurt-am-Main, 1963) pp. 155–205.
28. Cf. T. S. Eliot, 'The Metaphysical Poets', *Selected Prose of T. S. Eliot*, ed. Frank Kermode (London, 1975) p. 64.

29.   In *Schriften zum Theater*, *3*, pp. 182–3, Brecht makes his own connection between theatre and science.
30.   The theme is dominant in Stanislavski's work but see for example Constantin Stanislavski, *Creating a Role*, trs. Elizabeth Reynolds Hapgood (London, 1963) pp. 83–4.

Index

176

Index